GARDENS OF BRITAIN

GARDENS
OF
BRITAIN

John Gilbert

Executive Managers   Kelly Flynn
                             Susan Egerton-Jones
Art Editor   Ruth Levy
Production   Peter Phillips

Produced for W H Smith Ltd by the Artists House
Division of Mitchell Beazley International Ltd
Artists House
14–15 Manette Street
London W1V 5LB

Reprinted 1989

© Mitchell Beazley Publishers 1987

ISBN   0 86134 098 1

Typeset by Hourds Typographica, Stafford.
Reproduction by La Cromolito s.n.c., Milan.
Printed in Portugal by Printer Portuguesa, Lisbon

Contents

Introduction

The gardens of Britain, unsurpassed for beauty and variety, exemplify nature and art in the happiest of blends. Like the countryside itself, they are a continual source of pleasure and surprise with their contrasts and changing moods. No two are alike and no one of them is the same on successive visits. The transformations wrought by weather, time of day and season render their charms inexhaustible.

Terrain, soil and situation are of course determining factors. By and large, the gardens in the south-west of England, benefiting from a relatively mild climate throughout the year, display a greater profusion and diversity of plant growth than, say, northern England and Scotland. Even so, the natural shelter afforded by a hillside or valley, a wood or a sea cove, giving protection from frost and gales, often creates a microclimate that enables many tender, exotic and rare species to flourish outdoors in areas that most would consider unpromising. The fine gardens in the north prove that neither poor soil nor harshness of climate are necessarily a deterrent.

Natural conditions, however, are only the start. Gardens do not spring up overnight without a shaping hand, and even the wilderness effect must be shrewdly cultivated. Garden design and planning is a distinctively British talent, a combination of native skills and foreign influences. It presupposes a feeling for nature and an eye for artistic effect, a flair for innovation and improvization, a pride in individuality and even eccentricity.

No complete and original examples of Tudor gardens are still to be found, although certain features, such as the knot garden, have been reproduced, as at Hampton Court and, more convincingly, at Edzell Castle and Pitmedden in Scotland. There are relics of Elizabethan topiary and replicas of gazebos and mounts, as at Kew; but much has vanished or been destroyed. European influence, particularly from France, was strongly in evidence during the 17th century; and the inspiration of Versailles was unconcealed in many gardens of the day, complete with parterres, canals, pools and fountains, allées and avenues in neat geometrical patterns. Perhaps the best example of such a French-style garden is at Melbourne Hall. Early in the 18th century came a reaction against formality, and a return to nature was exemplified in the new landscape movement, eventually dominated by Kent, Brown and Repton. The emphasis was on distant vistas of woodland and water, with lawns sweeping down to lakes crossed by ornamental bridges, meandering paths and streams, and classical-style temples and statuary concealed in a grove or prominently positioned on a hill. The transition is well shown in the garden at Chiswick House, the pure landscape design is no better displayed than at Stourhead, and features of both old and new are juxtaposed at Chatsworth and Blenheim Palace.

The 19th century saw a return to formality, with Italian-style terracing, elaborate bedding schemes and impressive ornamental features, much of it in wrought iron. Tasteful and original examples of the new manner are the gardens at Alton Towers and Bodnant. The Victorians, in addition, were enthusiastic collectors, importing seeds from abroad and filling their gardens with flowers, shrubs and trees from all over the world, including North America, the Far East and the southern hemisphere.

The gardens of the present century have inherited the best characteristics of the past and have continued the practice of creating hybrids, growing new and rare plant species, and devising bold and attractive designs, often within a confined space. Much emphasis is nowadays placed on herbaceous borders and island beds, while the concept of open-air "rooms", introduced by Gertrude Jekyll, has been much adapted – most successfully in the gardens of Hidcote Manor and Sissinghurst Castle.

Other gardens have tended to specialize – in roses, rhododendrons and azaleas (Nymans is a splendid example), heathers, rock and alpine plants, trees (in several world-famous arboretums), etc. The great show gardens attached to research and teaching establishments (Wisley, Kew, Edinburgh, Springfields), invaluable both to professional and amateur gardeners, also afford infinite pleasure to all lovers of plants in a beautiful setting. The National Trusts for England and Scotland have been responsible for maintaining and restoring many lovely gardens for the benefit of their members and the wider public; while other properties, in private hands, reflect the individual tastes and talents of their owners.

This book describes about 200 gardens throughout Britain, many of them illustrated with specially commissioned colour photographs. With such a wealth of choice available, selection has not been easy, but, apart from obvious criteria such as intrinsic beauty and interest, care has been taken to find representative gardens from every part of the country which are readily accessible to the public. Some are open all year round, some daily in peak season, others only on certain days. Guidance has been given here as to days and months when particular gardens are open, but for up-to-date information on actual hours of opening, on entrance charges, catering and so forth, it is best to check by telephone beforehand as these details change frequently. Telephone numbers are obtainable from local directories, and the various national and regional tourist boards are always ready to help, as are local tourist offices. Gardens belonging to the National Trust (marked here by the symbol *NT*) are free to members, but a charge is normally made for other visitors.

For convenience the book has been divided broadly into traditional regions, moving up Britain from south to north. Within these regions gardens have been listed alphabetically under counties. The regional maps will also help motorists to locate the individual gardens.

LEWIS

OUTER HEBRIDES

NORTH
UIST

SKYE

SOUTH
UIST

INNER HEBRIDES

*ATLANTIC
OCEAN*

MULL

JURA

ISLAY

ARRAN

Firth of Clyde

HIGHLAND

GRAMPIAN

11 TAYSIDE

FIFE

CENTRAL

LOTHIAN

STRATH-
CLYDE

BORDERS

DUMFRIES &
GALLOWAY

NORTHUMBERLAND

TYNE & WEAR

DURHAM CLEVELAND

CUMBRIA

NORTH SEA

10

NORTH
YORKSHIRE

HUMBERSIDE

LANCS.

WEST
YORKS.

SOUTH
YORKS.

LONDONDERRY

12

ANTRIM

TYRONE

ARMAGH

COUNTY
DOWN

FERMANAGH

ISLE OF
MAN

GREATER
MANCHESTER

MERSEYSIDE

CHESHIRE

DERBYS.

NOTTS.

LINCS.

The Wash

7

NORFOLK

ANGLESEY

GWYNEDD

CLWYD

STAFFS.

SALOP

LEICS.

NORTHANTS.

CAMBS.

SUFFOLK

6

WEST
MIDLANDS

9

POWYS

8

WARKS.

BEDS.

HERTS.

ESSEX

HEREFORD &
WORCESTER

DYFED

W.
GLA
MORGAN

MID

S.

GWENT

GLOS.

5

OXON.

BUCKS.

4

THE REGIONS

1   The West Country
2   Southern England
3   South-East England
4   London
5   The Home Counties
6   East Anglia
7   East Midlands
8   West Midlands
9   Wales
10 Northern England
11 Scotland
12 Ulster

AVON

WILTS.

BERKS.

2

HANTS.

SURREY

WEST
SUSSEX

EAST
SUSSEX

KENT

3

Bristol Channel

SOMERSET

DORSET

ISLE OF
WIGHT

DEVON

1

CORNWALL

*ENGLISH
CHANNEL*

ISLES OF
SCILLY

7

The West Country

Avon Cornwall Devon Dorset Gloucestershire Somerset Wiltshire

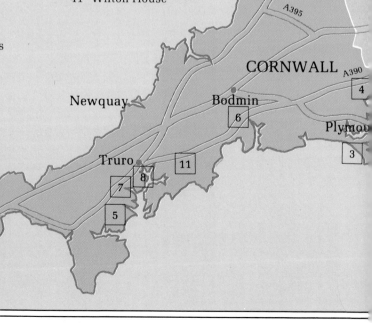

AVON
1 Claverton Manor
2 Dyrham Park

CORNWALL
3 Antony House
4 Cotehele House
5 Glendurgan
6 Lanhydrock
7 Penjerrick
8 Trelissick
9 Trengwainton
10 Tresco
11 Trewithen

DEVON
12 Bicton
13 Castle Drogo
14 Dartington Hall
15 Killerton
16 Knightshayes Court
17 Saltram House
18 Sharpitor

DORSET
19 Abbotsbury Sub-Tropical Gardens
20 Athelhampton
21 Compton Acres
22 Cranborne Manor
23 Forde Abbey

GLOUCESTERSHIRE
24 Barnsley House
25 Berkeley Castle
26 Hidcote Manor
27 Kiftsgate Court
28 Snowshill Manor
29 Sudeley Castle
30 Westbury Court
31 Westonbirt Arboretum

SOMERSET
32 Barrington Court
33 East Lambrook Manor
34 Hestercombe House
35 Lyte's Cary Manor
36 Montacute House
37 Tintinhull House

WILTSHIRE
38 Bowood
39 Corsham Court
40 Stourhead Garden
41 Wilton House

ISLES OF SCILLY

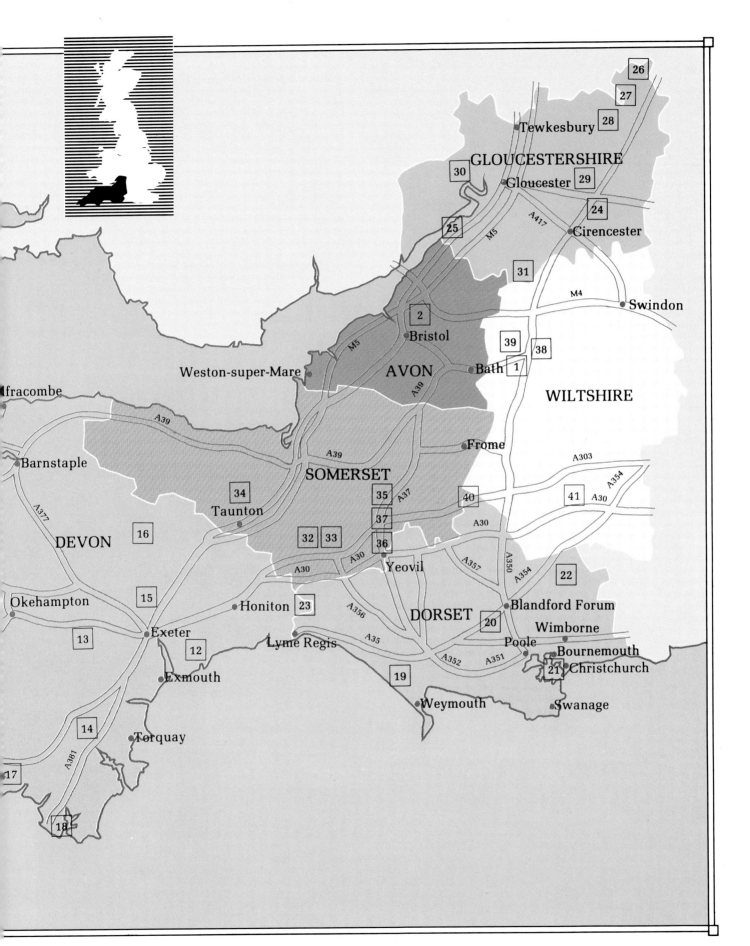

GLOUCESTERSHIRE

Tewkesbury

30

25

31

2

Bristol

AVON

Weston-super-Mare

Ifracombe

Barnstaple

SOMERSET

34

Taunton

DEVON

16

Okehampton

15

13

Exeter

12

Exmouth

14

Torquay

17

18

26

27

28

Gloucester 29

24

Cirencester

M5

A417

M4

Swindon

39

38

Bath 1

WILTSHIRE

Frome

A303

A354

35

A37

40

41

A30

37

32 33

36

Yeovil

A30

A357

A350

22

Honiton 23

A356

DORSET

20

Blandford Forum

Wimborne

Poole

Bournemouth

21

Christchurch

Swanage

Lyme Regis

A35

19

A352

A351

Weymouth

9

AVON

·1·
CLAVERTON MANOR
nr Bath

The old house accommodates the American Museum in Britain, but the garden mainly dates from 1960. There are attractive shrub and herbaceous borders, and a small colonial-style herb garden with a straw bee skep. Below is a rose and flower garden, with clipped box edges to the beds, trim gravel paths and a white fence. This is an accurate reproduction of George Washington's formal garden at Mount Vernon, Virginia.

Open April to Oct., Tues. to Sun.

Below: *Cotehele House.*

·2·
DYRHAM PARK
Chippenham

The late 17th-century stone mansion stands in 110 hectares (250 acres) of grounds. At that time the gardens, laid out by William Blathwayt in the grand formal manner, must have been impressive indeed, with a large parterre, terraces and walks, avenues of trees, fountains and basins. An immense cataract, some 15.25m (50ft) high, plunged down the hillside on the east front and into a conduit, flowing right under the house and re-emerging in the west garden, where all that remains of it today is a pool. It all made way for a landscape of considerable charm, though unadorned. Since 1961 Dyrham Park has been owned and continuously developed by the National Trust.

Garden open April to Oct.; April, May, Oct., Sat. to Wed.; June to Sept., daily except Fri. NT

CORNWALL

·3·
ANTONY HOUSE
Torpoint

The early 18th-century house, property of the National Trust since 1961, is surrounded by an extensive woodland garden. Humphry Repton worked here and some of the tree plantings are certainly his, although it is uncertain whether he was responsible for the radiating avenues through the full 360° of the compass which are among the most impressive sights here. Trees dominate the landscape, some of them old, some added more recently. They include a widely spreading hickory, numerous magnolias, a maidenhair tree or ginkgo, a cedar of Lebanon and some giant ilex. There are lawns and topiary specimens, including an immense yew arbour in the shape of a candle-snuffer.

Above: *Lanhydrock from the air.*

The oriental influence is very marked, both in the choice of plants and the ornamentation, with a fine Burmese temple bell at the end of one walk, flanked by Japanese stone lanterns, and Indian stone carvings. The rhododendrons and camellias are especially fine, and there is a good collection of hemerocallis or day lilies.

Garden open April to Oct., Tues. to Thurs. NT

· 4 ·

COTEHELE HOUSE
St Dominick, nr Callington

The National Trust administers this lovely garden in a glen, at the head of which is a beehive-shaped dovecote. It is steeply wooded, with a stream that cascades into a pool, and the rhododendrons, azaleas, and other flowering shrubs, are a riot of colour in spring. So are the bluebells and naturalized daffodils around the house, where there are lawns, flower beds and a little garden with a pool.

Open April to Oct., daily. NT

· 5 ·

GLENDURGAN
Mawnan Smith, nr Falmouth

This lovely National Trust garden, in a sheltered position across a narrow valley, leading down to the Helford River, benefits from a very mild climate and is renowned for a wide range of exotic trees and shrubs, including species from North and South America, Asia and Australia. These include rhododendrons in abundance, camellias, magnolias, eucryphias, hydrangeas, cornus species, bamboos, embothriums, tulip trees, loquats, myrtles, palms and the rare South American evergreen *Drimys winteri.* There is a rare weeping form of the Mexican Cypress, *Cupressus lusitanica,* and, on the upper lawn a splendid specimen of *Agave americana.* Planting of this garden in the glen probably began in the 1820s and one of the earliest additions was the unusual laurel maze, not symmetrical in shape and now with a whitebeam in the centre, planted on the steepest part of the slope of the valley, its pattern clearly discernible from the opposite side. In contrast to the semiwild character of other areas, there is a large walled garden near the house filled with bedding plants and climbers, including the New Zealand lobster claw, *Clianthus punicea, Acacia longifolia* and *A. dealbata,* and *Pittosporum tenuifolium* "Garnetti".

Garden open March to Oct., Mon., Wed., Fri. NT

· 6 ·

LANHYDROCK
nr Bodmin

The 17th-century house, later gutted by fire but skilfully reconstructed, is approached by a magnificent avenue which runs through the park. This originally consisted of sycamores, planted in 1648, but as these have aged and started to fall, they have gradually been replaced by beeches. In front of the house, with its adjoining church, is a highly ornate, two-storey 17th-century gatehouse in Gothic style to match the other buildings. The area bounded by house, church and gatehouse is made up of formal terraces surrounded by a low balustraded wall decorated with finials. The broad lawns are dotted at regular intervals with pyramids of clipped yew, and the neat flower beds, colourful throughout spring and summer, are edged with box hedges. The extremely elegant bronze urns are probably by Louis Ballin, who was goldsmith to Louis XIV.

The garden was given to the National Trust in 1955, and a recent addition is a

Right: *Trelissick.*
Far right: *Trengwainton.*

circular herbaceous garden surrounded by a hedge of clipped box and containing a good collection of bulbs and hardy plants.

The gardens above the house form a complete contrast, for they are wholly informal, both up the hillside and in the open parkland to the north. There is a delightful walk up a winding path through the woodland, where planting dates mainly from the present century, and from the top there are fine views of the house and gardens below. Here in profusion are the trees and splendid flowering shrubs for which Lanhydrock is rightly famous. The trees include Irish yews, Sitka spruce and Douglas fir. In spring the magnolias, some of them over 15m (50ft) tall, are in their full glory, continuing in flower until June. Especially lovely are the early-flowering *Magnolia campbellii* and *M. mollicomata*, and later *M. veitchii* and *M. soulangiana*. These are freely mingled with rhododendrons, especially hardy hybrids, azaleas, camellias and hydrangeas. Maples and other broad-leaved trees provide rich foliage colour in autumn.

Garden open all year, daily. NT

· 7 ·
PENJERRICK
Budock, Falmouth

The copper beeches at Penjerrick are especially fine, and there are many other splendid trees in this warm and sheltered garden, including eucryphias, Irish yews, magnolias and weeping beech. But the garden is renowned also for its superb rhododendrons, including the "Penjerrick" and "Cornish Cross" hybrids, and many other cream, white and pink forms raised here.

Open March to Sept., Sun., Wed.

· 8 ·
TRELISSICK
Truro

This lovely woodland garden, maintained since 1935 by the National

Trust, enjoys a sheltered position above the estuary of the River Fal, lying on either side of a valley and road down to the King Harry Ferry. It was originally planted with trees and shrubs by Mr and Mrs Ronald Copeland. He was managing director of the Spode china factory and many of the flowers painted on Copeland china were grown in his garden. Wide lawns slope down to the valley, and the hydrangeas surrounding them are a wonderful sight in late summer. The rhododendrons and azaleas, too, are enormously varied, as are the camellias and other flowering shrubs. The spring bulbs and summer borders help to provide a continuity of colour.

The many fine trees include oaks, beeches, Japanese and deodar cedars, holm oaks, maritime pines and some enormous cryptomerias (incense cedars).

Garden open March to Oct., daily. NT

· 9 ·
TRENGWAINTON
Heamoor, nr Penzance

Owned by the Bolitho family and administered since 1961 by the National Trust, this is one of the most interesting of all Cornish gardens, with an unrivalled collection of exotic plants. The layout is unusual for it comprises two principal sections, a series of brick-walled gardens by the entrance lodge, linked by a long drive and stream garden to the lawns and garden around the house. Each of the five walled enclosures contains a choice selection of trees and shrubs, some of them tender and rare, including many species of magnolia, eucalyptus, eucryphias, acacias, rhododendrons, etc. The drive to the house is densely planted with rhododendrons and other shrubs, and the stream garden that runs parallel has innumerable water-loving plants — primulas, meconopsis, astilbes, arum lilies, tree ferns, etc.

Garden open March to Oct., Wed. to Sat. NT

DEVON

·10·
TRESCO ABBEY GARDENS
Tresco, Isles of Scilly

Special feature – see page 14.

·11·
TREWITHEN
Probus

This is yet another splendid Cornish garden with a marvellous collection of mature plants in a beautifully designed woodland setting. The walled garden beside the house contains a huge lobster claw plant and other choice climbers. The woodland garden around the long, tapering lawn is full of rhododendrons, including the "Trewithen Orange" hybrid, evergreen azaleas, camellias, embothriums and Asiatic magnolias, a speciality of the late owner Mr George Johnstone. Beyond the lawn is a dell with moist and protected conditions for tree ferns and other shrubs. As is the case with other gardens in Cornwall, the mild climate encourages the growth of many tender species too numerous to mention. There are also water gardens and a rose garden.

Garden open April to Sept., daily except Sun.

·12·
BICTON
nr Budleigh Salterton

The gardens at Bicton, extending over 50 acres, are set well away from the house. There are, in fact, three distinct garden areas, the Italian Garden, the American Garden and the Pinetum. The first of these is formal, beautifully designed and proportioned, in the 18th-century style of Le Nôtre. Encircled by brick walls, its central feature is a rectangular pond flanked on three sides by smaller canal pools, with a tall three-basined fountain. The grass parterre is adorned with lead figures on pedestals, and steps lead up a grassy ridge to an upper terrace, the principal feature of which is a row of ornamental greenhouses, with an open central area known as the Temple, framed by two huge cedars. In these glasshouses, and in the handsome Palm House situated in a small garden near by, is a splendid collection of tropical and temperate plants.

The American garden, originally created to accommodate trees and shrubs from North America, contains rhododendrons, azaleas and some fine trees, including Mexican pines. There is also an unusual Shell House, with exhibits mainly from the Caribbean.

The Pinetum is one of the most impressive in the country. It dates from 1840 and includes a magnificent avenue of araucarias (monkey-puzzles). Among the many specimen trees, some of them of immense height, are *Abies cephalonica*, the rare *A. squamata*, *Athrotaxis cupressoides*, *Chamaecyparis lawsoniana*, *Cryptomeria japonica*, *Pinus ponderosa*, *P. coulteri*, *Podocarpus macrophyllus* and *Quercus phellos*, to mention only a very few.

Beyond the Pinetum is a rustic summerhouse, built in 1839, its floor made of the knuckle bones of deer and the outside covered with wooden shingles. It is called the Hermitage.

The gardens, including the Pinetum, can be seen from the covered and open coaches of a narrow-gauge railway.

Gardens open March to Oct., daily.

·10·
Tresco Abbey Gardens

Tresco, Isles of Scilly

In 1834 Mr Augustus Smith acquired the lease of the barren, windswept Isles of Scilly in the Atlantic, 40 miles off the tip of Cornwall. Near the site of an ancient abbey he built his house and proceeded to create around it a garden which is today unique in the British Isles. He filled the garden with many exotic and rare species, mainly from the southern hemisphere, and because of the ideal climate, thanks largely to the warming influence of the Gulf Stream, and so virtually frost-free, these plants grew and continue to grow in profusion, as nowhere else in Britain.

Augustus Smith planted windbreaks of Monterey cypress and Monterey pine from California, made tall hedges of holm oak, and built strong granite walls. The garden was laid out in terraces on the windward side of a small hill. He then filled it with an immensely varied collection of plants, with an emphasis on species from Australia, New Zealand, South Africa, Central and South America, and the Canary Islands.

These plants, over a century later, present an unrivalled spectacle of subtropical luxuriance, and although difficult to get to (helicopter or boat from the mainland to St Mary's and then by ferry), the garden is well worth a special visit.

The central lengthwise axis of the garden is

Far left: the head of the sea
god at the top of the Neptune
Steps.
Left: the Long Walk, with its
luxuriant vegetation.
Above: figureheads in the
Valhalla Museum.
Below left: arch of the Old
Abbey.

formed by the lowest of the three terraces, the
Long Walk. Above and parallel, following the
contours of the hillside, are the Middle Terrace
and the Top Terrace, connected, as in the rest of
the garden, by paths. Running at right-angles to
the terraces is the Lighthouse Walk, terminating in the Neptune Steps which lead up to a
stone head of the sea god.

The plants that grow everywhere, along the
terraces, in the orchards and rockeries, and over
the walls are obviously impossible to list in a
brief survey; because of their special interest
and frequent rarity, care has been taken to label
them all clearly. They include many species of
aeonium, with rosettes of yellow or pink
flowers; agaves, with one giant form from
Mexico; brightly coloured succulents known
collectively as mesembryanthemums; giant
echiums, dazzling blue and mauve in spring and
early summer; banksias from Australia; pelargo-
niums; and species of protea from South Africa.

The numerous imposing trees include palms,
acacias, eucalyptus, an araucaria now more
than 30m (100ft) high, a rare Kauri pine also of
huge dimensions, a grove of *Myrtus luna* from
Chile, rare forms of *Leucodendron*, the rata
from New Zealand, with bright scarlet blooms,
and the New Zealand evergreen *Griselliria
littoralis.*

The woodland approach to the house is
worth the detour and an additional special
feature is the little Valhalla Museum at the
south entrance. This contains a fascinating
collection of figureheads, since restored and
repainted, from old ships wrecked off the
islands.

Gardens open all year, daily.

Right: *Knightshayes Court, topiary.*

· 13 ·
CASTLE DROGO
Drewsteignton

Sir Edwin Lutyens built this extraordinary granite, medieval-style castle high on the fringe of Dartmoor, overlooking the gorge of the River Teign, between 1910 and 1920. It was acquired by the National Trust in 1975. The terraced gardens are enclosed by yew hedges, and were to have been planted by Gertrude Jekyll, but her ideas were not accepted. Steps lead up two terrace levels through rose beds and herbaceous borders, then past shrub borders and finally to a vast circular lawn flanked by cypresses. It is all starkly formal and, in its bleak surroundings, as surprising and impressive as the building itself.

Open April to Oct., daily. NT

· 14 ·
DARTINGTON HALL
nr Totnes

The lovely stone house dates in parts from the 14th century, but the garden is mostly modern, the work of an American, Mrs Beatrix Farrand, before World War II, and of Percy Cane in postwar years. The main garden is on the site of the ancient tiltyard belonging to the builder of Dartington, John Holland, Duke of Exeter, a famous jouster. Stone steps and terraces lead down into an open-air amphitheatre with a balustraded walk, and another broad flight of steps at the opposite end leads to a lawn which was originally the tournament ground. Here is a line of Irish yews known as the Twelve Apostles, a splendid Monterey pine, seven very old sweet chestnuts and a statue of a reclining woman by Henry Moore, one of the several examples of contemporary sculpture in the gardens.

The extensive area beyond the tournament ground consists of woodland and meadow, with an azalea dell. The woodland walks are delightful, with bulbs, shrubs and trees to provide interest and colour at all seasons.

Garden open all year, daily.

· 15 ·
KILLERTON
Broadclyst, nr Exeter

Killerton, the property of the Acland family and owned since 1944 by the National Trust, is mainly noted for one of the earliest collections of trees in Britain, much of it planted by John Veitch, who subsequently founded the Exeter nursery firm. The terrace to the south of the house is the only formal feature, with beds planted for year-round colour, and some decorative urns. The arboretum lies high on a hillside, and the zigzag path goes past a quaint rustic summerhouse known as the Bear's Hut, the floor being laid with knucklebones of deer. The woods are notable for many magnificent conifers, including wellingtonias, Lawson cypresses, spruces and pines, many fine oaks and maples, magnolias, and banks of rhododendrons and azaleas.

Garden open all year, daily. NT

· 16 ·
KNIGHTSHAYES COURT
Tiverton

The 19th-century house is situated on a hillside above the valley of the River Exe, but with the exception of some yew hedges and mature trees, the garden is young, having been created since the end of World War II by Sir John and Lady Heathcoat Amory. The existing formal gardens were completely transformed and the extensive woodland area was similarly altered and enlarged to accommodate a splendid selection of exotic plants. The skilful design and imaginative planting have made this one of the most charming gardens in the south-west, and since Sir John's death in 1972 it has been maintained jointly by the Knightshayes Trust and the National Trust.

The formal gardens exhibit many fascinating features. The old bowling green is now a grass parterre enclosed by yew hedges, with a large, circular stone-edged pool, a single white statue in a yew alcove, and a silver weeping pear. On the other side of a gravel path is another little garden with a topiary pattern around the top of the yew hedge which depicts hounds chasing a fox. A third enclosure is a parterre planted in shades of purple, grey and silver.

The formal garden blends gradually with the main woodland area beyond. This lovely "Garden in the Wood" has been greatly expanded over the years, the overcrowded parts thinned out and many new species of shrubs introduced. Long island beds are separated by grass paths and many are edged with raised peat blocks to protect the plants.

Tall trees form a canopy over this woodland garden which glows with colour at every season. There are splendid magnolias, pieris, rhododendrons and azaleas, climbing roses, and a rich miscellany of more modest plants including violets, hellebores, hostas, lilies and ferns, to mention only a few, providing virtually unbroken ground cover. The range of herbaceous species is quite astonishing, far greater than in many other woodland gardens.

Open end-March to Oct., daily. NT

· 17 ·
SALTRAM HOUSE
Plympton, nr Plymouth

The Georgian house stands in an 18th-century landscape park. There are many fine trees and a long lime avenue. At the top of the garden is an octagonal summerhouse known as the "Castle". The handsome wood-framed orangery, built in 1775, was destroyed by fire but restored in 1961 by the National Trust. Ornamental tubs containing oranges are moved outside each summer. In the woods below is a little stone temple called "Fanny's Bower", after Fanny Burney, the diarist, who stayed at Saltram with the Royal Family in 1789.

Open all year, daily. NT

· 18 ·
SHARPITOR
Salcombe

Administered by the National Trust, this small garden, with splendid rhododendrons, azaleas, magnolias and beautiful flowering plants that flourish in the mild maritime surroundings, is steeply terraced and commands a dramatic view over the Salcombe estuary. There are numerous palms and, in the lower garden, a splendid *Magnolia campbellii.*

Garden open all year, daily. NT

DORSET

· 19 ·
ABBOTSBURY SUB-TROPICAL GARDENS
Abbotsbury

The large woodland garden containing the fine collection of sub-tropical plants begun by Lord Ilchester about 1815 slopes down to the sea. The big walled garden is especially well maintained and has immense camellias, rhododendrons, magnolias, mimosas and palms. Elsewhere the trees and shrubs are densely planted, with splendid specimens of acacias, Chilean myrtles, hydrangeas, cordylines and innumerable other species which thrive in the exceptionally mild surroundings.

Open mid-March to mid-Oct., daily.

· 20 ·
ATHELHAMPTON
Puddletown

Although the house is Tudor, the garden is modern, laid out in 1891 and continuously enlarged and developed since. It has all been done, however, to match the style of the house, with six walled enclosures, tall hedges, topiary, stonework, wrought iron gates, parterres, pools, fountains, statuary and ornaments. One of the larger enclosures is backed by a stone terrace and flanking pavilions; another has a small pool with obelisk-topped walls; and a third has topiary peafowl and a lion's head fountain. Each garden has individual character and beauty. A path leads to the more recently planted informal gardens beside the River Piddle which encircles the house, with flower borders and semi-wild areas with shrubs and moisture-loving plants. An interesting feature is an old dovecote, recently restored, on a lawn backed by an alley of yews.

Garden open end-March to mid-Oct., Wed., Thurs., Sun., also Mon., Tues. in Aug.

· 21 ·
COMPTON ACRES
Canford Cliffs, Poole

Thomas William Simpson created this very popular series of gardens, each in a different style, between the wars. It was a moorland site and he spent lavishly to landscape it, bringing in stone and rock, planting it with exotic shrubs and trees, and decorating it with ornaments and statuary to create his special effects of period, place and style. The English garden around the house has lawns, flower borders and rose beds. The Italian garden contains a large canal pool, classical statues, terraces and a small temple. There is a small Roman garden, a heather dell which also accommodates rhododendrons and azaleas, a palm court with elaborate statuary, a rock and water garden with pools and rustic bridges, and – a particular attraction with visitors – a Japanese garden. This is authentically designed and planted, with a tea-house, a temple, carved lanterns, a statue of Buddha, ornamental gateways and water features. It was restored and opened to the public in 1952.

Garden open April to Oct., daily.

· 22 ·
CRANBORNE MANOR
Cranborne

This beautiful stone manor house was acquired by Robert Cecil, later Earl of Salisbury, in the early 17th century. Although he paid more attention to his other property, Hatfield House, he laid out a fine garden at Cranborne with the aid of the renowned John Tradescant. Of this garden the bowling-alley and mount still survive, although the latter is now only a few feet high and laid out as a rose garden.

The entrance is down a steep gravelled drive and under an arch which links two square lodges, and the court beyond, with climbing plants on the walls as well as up the front of the house, is full of roses, pinks and other sweetly scented flowers. Overlooking this terrace, on the north facade of the house, is a classical porch, possibly by Inigo Jones, and there is another on the south front.

The garden was neglected for two centuries and then renovated by the Second Marquis of Salisbury. After World War II the Sixth Marquis and his wife replanted it, accentuating the formality and giving it something of the open-air "room" effect of Sissinghurst. There is a knot garden leading to the mount, a white garden, a streamside garden, an old kitchen garden and an avenue of pleached limes. But the most original section, separated from the other parts and wholly enclosed by walls, is a charming medieval-style herb garden, with orderly beds containing not only herbs but also a wide selection of sweetly scented plants.

The herbaceous borders provide a continuity of seasonal colour, and dominating the overall garden scheme is the imposing manor itself with its rose-clad walls.

A recent addition is the garden centre, selling many of the unusual plants grown there.

Open March to Oct., Wed. only.

· 23 ·
FORDE ABBEY
nr Chard

The 12th-century Cistercian monastery is surrounded by 25 acres of lovely gardens. Beyond the long canal in front of the building is a woodland garden with fine rhododendrons and magnolias, and a bog garden with primulas, astilbes, irises, ferns and other moisture-loving species. On the far side of a pond planted with water lilies is a remarkable summerhouse, every part of which is made of living beech. Elsewhere there are good shrubs and herbaceous plants, a rock garden, a kitchen garden and nursery, and a garden centre.

Open April to Oct., Mon. to Fri.

GLOUCESTERSHIRE

· 24 ·
BARNSLEY HOUSE
Barnsley, nr Cirencester

The garden of Barnsley House, although quite small, covering only some two-and-a-half acres, is a happy blend of the formal and informal, largely created since 1951 by Mr and Mrs David Verey. Planting throughout, on walls, along paths, in borders and in containers, has been carried out with a fastidious eye for form and colour, with

delightfully harmonious associations, and the entire garden is a haven of grace and tranquillity.

The house, built of grey stone, dates from 1697 and was given a third storey with a castellated roof, as well as a Gothic colonnaded verandah, in the early 19th century. The front of the house is terraced, with a stretch of lawn sweeping up to a charming Gothic summerhouse built in 1762 by the Rev. Charles Coxwell for his wife, when the house was a rectory. This is the focal point of what is virtually a picturesque miniature landscape.

One of the principal attractions of the post-war garden designed by the Vereys is the grass walk with a late 18th-century Doric temple at one end. In front of the temple is a pond and a little paved garden enclosed by a wrought-iron screen. At the other end of the walk is a modern fountain in Purbeck stone by Simon Verity. On one side of the walk are mixed flower borders and on the other an arcade of laburnums. Crossing the walk is a path with Irish yews which leads to a grass and flower parterre, and in front of the Gothic verandah is a recently planted knot garden with box, lavender, rosemary and many species grown in Elizabethan times. These is also a small arboretum, still developing but already

Above: *Forde Abbey.*
Right: *Kiftsgate Court, pool and fountain.*

full of spring and autumn colour, and a kitchen garden laid out as a potager.

Garden open all year. Wed., weekdays May to Sept.

· 25 ·
BERKELEY CASTLE
Berkeley

The garden of this beautiful 12th-century castle is fairly simple, dating almost wholly from the present century. There are some excellent shrubs and climbers along the terrace-like battlements on two sides of the castle, and planting everywhere has been very skilful, with a good eye for colour associations. Special features include a water lily pond, an old bowling alley and a butterfly house.

Open April to Sept., daily except Mon.; Oct., Sun. only.

· 26 ·
HIDCOTE MANOR
Hidcote Bartrim, nr Mickleton

Special feature – see page 20.

· 27 ·
KIFTSGATE COURT
Mickleton

This charming garden is situated very close to Hidcote. Although not as consciously designed, nor as varied, as its more famous neighbour, it is a quiet, intimate place and well worth visiting. The two rectangular gardens on different sides of the house are individually treated. One has a pool and fountain and is planted predominantly in silver and white; the other has four box-edged beds of shrubs. Between them is a wide grass path with superb double mixed borders. Below the house, terraces and paths slope steeply down to a flight of steps that leads to a lawn and pool. Kiftsgate is luxuriantly planted and always colourful, especially in summer when the roses are in bloom.

Garden open April to Sept., Wed., Thurs., Sun.

· 28 ·
SNOWSHILL MANOR
Broadway

This charming little garden, set around a fine Tudor mansion, is attractively terraced on various levels, and the separate garden "rooms" are divided by walls, steps and arches, with fountains and ponds, niches and troughs, a dovecote and much else to provide extra interest. Design was all important to Charles Wade in 1919 and he may well have been influenced by a visit to nearby Hidcote. At Snowshill, too, the National Trust has lovingly maintained the original artistic and architectural

conception. The place is delightful.

Open May to Sept., daily except Mon. and Tues. April and Oct., Sat., Sun. NT

· 29 ·
SUDELEY CASTLE
Winchcombe, nr Cheltenham Spa

The lovely castle, of Cotswold stone, was sacked in Cromwell's time and partially restored in the 19th century, but the ruined parts enhance the beauty of the garden. There are broad lawns, shrub borders, clipped yews, many fine trees (including a Judas tree and some immense walnuts), and an Elizabethan-style herb garden. A lily pond is surrounded by stone balustrades and weeping pears. The waterfowl collection is an additional attraction.

Open April to Oct., daily.

· 30 ·
WESTBURY COURT
Westbury on Severn

This is a Dutch-style late 17th-century water garden, long neglected and beautifully reconstructed and restored by the National Trust during the 1970s. The central features are two adjacent canals, one straight, with a two-storey pavilion at its head, the other wider and T-shaped, with a statue of Neptune at the intersections. Both canals are surrounded by clipped yew hedges and lawns. There is a little walled garden which has been replanted with hundreds of species of plants grown before 1700, including old roses, herbs and medicinal plants, bulbs, shrubs and fruit trees. The restoration was based on original plans and accounts and approximates as closely as possible to the original garden.

Garden open April to Oct., Wed. to Sun. NT

· 31 ·
WESTONBIRT ARBORETUM
Westonbirt

Begun by Robert Staynor Holford in 1829, steadily enlarged by members of

·26·
Hidcote Manor

Hidcote Bartrim, nr Mickleton, Gloucestershire

This lovely 4-hectare (10-acre) garden was created about 80 years ago by the American owner of the adjoining farmhouse, Major Lawrence Johnston. Although beautifully situated in the rolling Cotswold hills, the site was bleak and unpromising, its principal features being a solitary cedar of Lebanon and a clump of five beech trees. Major Johnston began by planting windbreaks in the form of criss-crossed hedges. Some of these were yew but others were less conventional, made up of mingled yew and box or, even more ambitiously, in a "tapestry" of yew, beech and holly. Furthermore, these hedges were used in an individual and imaginative way to partition small areas of garden, either enclosed or largely open, thus creating outdoor "rooms" in a manner that later became fashionable and popular, but which was at that period a novelty.

The central axis of the garden, running the entire length like the corridor of a house, is a long, narrow alley, itself subdivided into little garden sections. On either side of this main walk are other small, self-contained gardens, some planted for colour, others simpler with a feature such as a pond. Lawrence Johnston was a discerning plant collector and he designed his garden at Hidcote with an eye for natural beauty, botanical interest and artistic effect. His original ideas were faithfully followed by the National Trust which acquired the property in 1948 when, after the neglect caused by the war, considerable restoration was needed.

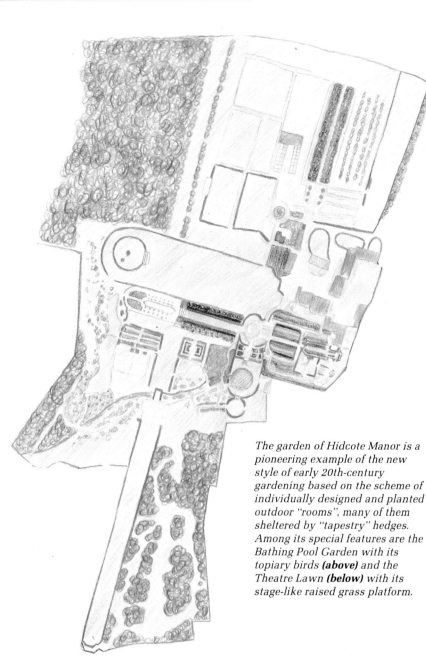

The garden of Hidcote Manor is a pioneering example of the new style of early 20th-century gardening based on the scheme of individually designed and planted outdoor "rooms", many of them sheltered by "tapestry" hedges. Among its special features are the Bathing Pool Garden with its topiary birds **(above)** *and the Theatre Lawn* **(below)** *with its stage-like raised grass platform.*

The pattern of this relatively small garden is quite complex but there are two immediately striking features. One is the central walk which leads from the area dominated by the original cedar, through sections planted in various colour combinations (one in reds, oranges and bronze) to a flight of steps flanked by little pavilions and a double line of clipped hornbeams on bare trunks, giving them the illusion of standing on stilts; this leads on to the wrought-iron gates that form the boundary of the garden, through which there are delightful views of the countryside. The second dramatic feature, parallel to the main alley, is a large, rectangular area of turf, the Theatre Lawn, surrounded by a yew hedge, with the ancient beeches standing on a stage-like grassy platform at the far end.

Elsewhere narrow paths link the individual gardens, each of which makes its impact by virtue of bold or harmonious colour combinations, or by simplicity of design. The fuchsia garden is surrounded by "tapestry" hedges. The pool garden, enclosed by cropped yew hedges, consists of a circular, raised lily pond, and another has a stone basin formerly used as a bathing pool, with an adjoining hedged area for a dressing room. The rose garden contains many old shrub roses which were much admired by Vita Sackville-West, who created another world-famous garden, on similar principles, at Sissinghurst. Mrs Winthrop's garden, named after Major Johnston's mother, is planted with yellow and blue flowers, while other sections are in orange and yellow, silver and gold, and – alongside a natural streamside garden – in subtle shades of green, lime, yellow and bronze. There is a garden with pillars of yew, another with Dutch-style topiary, and yet another with shrubs and ground cover species.

Hidcote is a joy for the ordinary visitor and provides a wealth of interest for gardeners with a love for unusual plants and an appreciation for bold and original design.

Garden open April to Oct., daily except Tues., Fri. NT

the Holford family and maintained since 1956 by the Forestry Commission, Westonbirt Arboretum is Britain's oldest and largest tree collection which, with the Silk Wood annexe, covers over 60.75 hectares (150 acres). It is laid out on a fairly simple pattern of broad grassy drives which enclose blocks of trees, interspersed with open spaces and glades. Yet apart from its immense scientific interest, Westonbirt is also a woodland garden of incomparable variety and great beauty. The trees provide a wealth of colour at all seasons, including winter, and hosts of rhododendrons, azaleas, magnolias and cherries add charm in spring and early summer. One of the most popular areas is planted with Japanese maples, providing spectacular leaf tints in autumn.

Arboretum open all year, daily.

SOMERSET

· 32 ·
BARRINGTON COURT
Ilminster

The beautiful Tudor house in Ham stone, property of the National Trust since 1907, is encircled by a moat and surrounded by lawns, meadows and avenues of horse chestnuts. The nearby 17th-century stable block, in red brick, with other outbuildings, is the setting for a series of linked walled gardens, some of them designed, though never seen, by Gertrude Jekyll in her old age. Each has its individual character and planting scheme, providing an overall effect of lavish colour. They include a kitchen garden, a rose garden with a central statue, an iris garden which also contains lavender and purple clematis, with a stepped sundial, and a lily garden with high brick walls, a brickwork path, a central pool with raised beds, and wide flower borders, with crinum lilies and azaleas.

Garden open April to Sept., Sun. to Wed. NT

· 33 ·
EAST LAMBROOK MANOR
South Petherton

This lovely cottage-style garden was made in 1937 by the late Margery Fish and her husband around their 15th-century house, and is a marvellous example of natural gardening, with many rare and unusual plants. All-season colour from the shrubs and flowers is beautifully supplemented by the foliage of some interesting trees, including a fine variegated sycamore on the back lawn. There is a silver garden, a woodland garden, a green garden with grasses and green flowers.

Garden open early Jan. to late Dec., daily.

· 34 ·
HESTERCOMBE HOUSE
Cheddon Fitzpaine, Taunton

This early 20th-century garden stems from the collaboration of the architect Sir Edwin Lutyens and the garden designer Gertrude Jekyll. Terraces and raised walks surround a sunken parterre, which is the central feature, and there are many fine examples of Lutyens's bold and imaginative use of stonework, including a long pillared pergola, which complements and highlights the various planting schemes.

Open all year, Tues. and Thurs. and last Suns. of May to July.

· 35 ·
LYTE'S CARY MANOR
nr Ilchester

The medieval manor house belonged to Sir Henry Lyte, who in 1578 published his *Herball*, mainly concerning the medicinal value of plants, and referring briefly to his own house. His family were keen gardeners but nothing is known of their work. The present garden dates from the early part of the present century, having been created by Sir Walter Jenner, and maintained since 1949 by the National Trust. The house is approached by a fine avenue of pleached limes, and the pattern is a series of small gardens, including an Old English garden and a rose garden,

with attractive yew topiary, box hedges, alleys, a lily pool and garden statuary.

Open April to end Oct., Wed., Sat. NT

· 36 ·
MONTACUTE HOUSE
Yeovil

This lovely Elizabethan house of locally quarried Ham stone has a relatively modern garden and is something of an oddity because in the course of centuries it has been turned back to front. The present entrance along a drive flanked by Irish yews, cedars, limes and beeches, is on the west side, whereas the original front entrance, to the east, has since been converted into a pleasant garden of lawn and flower borders.

The present garden was begun about 150 years ago by Ellen Phelips, wife of the then owner, and her gardener, Mr Pridham. They laid out grass parterres and planted yew hedges on the north side of the house, replacing the ancient mount with a balustraded lily pool. This remains the central feature of a simple and elegant sunken garden, which also has a fountain, added later, and a raised terrace leading to an orangery.

Montacute was given to the National Trust in 1931, which after World War II called in Vita Sackville West, who designed the garden of Sissinghurst Castle, to plan the east forecourt borders, which she planted with roses, shrubs, climbers and perennials.

Garden open end March to Oct., daily. NT

· 37 ·
TINTINHULL HOUSE
nr Yeovil

The garden of this small 17th-century manor house, with a lovely west front added in the reign of Queen Anne, dates only from 1933. Less than an acre in size, it was created by Mrs Phyllis Reiss who gave it to the National Trust in 1953. Basically it is several gardens in one, each distinctive in character and highly original both in design and planting. The largest comprises a stretch of lawn dominated by yews and

Above: *Tintinhull House.*

---

a many-limbed cedar of Lebanon, and a mixed border with roses, peonies, magnolias, lilac and herbaceous perennials. This leads to a flower garden, with plants in borders and containers and a central canal pool and a pillared summerhouse.

From the low balustraded terrace, with its benches and tubs of plants, a long, straight path of geometrically patterned flagstones runs down to a wall of clipped yews, but on either side of the path, which is lined by low, neatly trimmed cones of box, are smaller gardens. Immediately below the terrace is the Eagle Court, so named because the piers of the walls protecting this little flower garden are surmounted by eagles. The next section is dominated by a huge holm oak, and at the far end is a tiny paved parterre and lily pool.

The whole garden is a perfect setting for the elegant house, built of local honey-coloured stone, and is a model of simplicity, with immense variety thanks to mixed planting, a wealth of colour in spring and summer, and all within a comparatively confined area.

Garden open April to Sept., Mon., Wed., Thurs., Sat. NT

WILTSHIRE

· 38 ·
BOWOOD
Calne

This characteristic and very beautiful "Capability" Brown landscape dates from 1761. In typical manner, Brown dammed the valley below the house to form a lake, surrounded it with clumps and belts of trees, and placed a single small classical temple on a promontory on the far bank. A mossy cascade, 10m (35ft) high, and a grotto were added in 1785. Italian-style terraces were built around the house in the mid-19th century, and these have been kept quite simple, giving an impressive view over the park landscape. New trees in the park have also been planted outside the landscape so as not to spoil the effect. They include firs, Lawson cypresses, redwoods and cedars. Colour is provided in spring by daffodils and bluebells, and in summer by splendid rhododendrons, azaleas and roses. There is also a garden centre.

Garden open April to Sept., daily.

· 39 ·
CORSHAM COURT
Corsham

The park and gardens of this Elizabethan manor were laid out by "Capability" Brown, who made a large lake, planted numerous trees and built a bath house, mainly for an ornamental purpose. Humphry Repton later transformed this landscape, enlarging the lake, planting an elm avenue and engaging John Nash to add a pinnacled facade to the bath house. In the mid-19th century a tall serpentine wall was put up to resemble a ruin, and then a flower garden was added. The roses and herbaceous border are attractive.

Open mid-Jan. to mid-Dec., daily except Fri., Mon.

· 40 ·
STOURHEAD GARDEN
Stourton

Special feature – see page 24.

· 41 ·
WILTON HOUSE
Wilton

Drawings indicate that the gardens of Wilton House, home of the Earls of Pembroke, were once very elaborate and imposing, but what the visitor sees today is a mixture of styles from the 18th century to the present day. The parkland setting comprises some 8 hectares (20 acres) of lawn alongside the little River Nadder, which was dammed and widened to become a central feature of the early 18th-century landscape. Some of the immense cedars of Lebanon, which constitute a principal feature of the garden today, may have been planted even before this time, and other notable specimen trees include oaks, planes, limes and tulip trees. The handsome Palladian bridge over the river dates from 1737 and was designed by Roger Morris. The forecourt of the house was transformed by David Vicary in 1971 into a formal garden enclosed by pleached limes, with flower beds and a splendid jet fountain.

Garden open late March to mid-Oct., daily except Mon.

·40·
Stourhead Garden

Stourton, Wiltshire

Stourhead is one of the first landscape gardens in Britain, begun before "Capability" Brown embarked seriously on his professional career, and unquestionably one of the most beautiful.

The banker Henry Hoare bought Stourton House in 1714, pulled it down and built his new house four years later. It was his son Henry, a classical scholar, who inherited the property and started to lay out the present gardens in 1744. He dammed the little River Stour which flowed through the bare valley and created a series of lakes, the biggest of which formed the centrepiece of a landscape garden conceived as a true work of art. The sides of the valley were

planted with beech and fir, the masses of dark and pale green deliberately contrasted as in a painting, and at various points along the path surrounding the lake with its wooden bridge, a number of small classical-style buildings formed focal points for delightful vistas. Everything was precisely planned for maximum effect, and the result was the natural equivalent of the setting for a painting by Claude or Poussin.

The owner had intended his guests to begin their tour of the gardens from the house, but visitors today start at the lower end near the village. The first building passed is the Temple of Flora, suitably dedicated to the Roman goddess of flowers and spring, its facade of pillars framed in a leafy arbour. The Grotto, a favourite feature of landscape garden design, is particularly impressive; steps lead down to a rocky underground cavern, with natural light filtering through from an opening above, where, in an alcove a stone nymph lies on a rocky couch watered by a spring. Beyond is another carving of the sea god, Neptune. Emerging into the daylight once more, the visitor climbs up to a charming rustic cottage, and then reaches the porticoed Pantheon, a miniature version of its

famous namesake in Rome, containing statues of gods and heroes. The path now zigzags up the hill to the Temple of Apollo, with splendid views over the whole landscape, including the Obelisk commemorating the Hoare family on the far side of the lake. Finally there is a descent to the Stone Bridge and the circuit is complete.

One further monument which predates the neo-classical buildings is the tall Market Cross, discovered by Henry Hoare abandoned in a Bristol builders' yard and set up, beautifully restored, at Stourhead.

No matter which starting point is taken, or which direction, the views are beguiling and continuously varied according to weather and season. In spring the daffodils bob by the lakeside and soon the rhododendrons – the result of much later planting – are in full glory. In summer the hydrangeas make a fine mass of colour and the trees, which are truly Stourhead's chief pride, frame the lake in every shade of green. But for many the gardens are most to be enjoyed on a quiet day in autumn when the russet, red and gold of the foliage forms the loveliest setting for this magnificent showplace.

Garden open all year, daily. NT

Stourhead, one of the first landscape gardens in England, is notable for its architectural features.
Top left: *the lead statue by Rysbrack of Neptune, inside the Grotto.*
Far left, below: *view across the turf bridge and the lake of the Pantheon, built in the mid-18th century by Henry Flitcroft. The portico is shown bottom right.*
Below left: *the woodland path around the lake.*
Below: *the Temple of Flora, one of the earliest of Henry Hoare's classical features, built above the village spring.*

Southern England

Hampshire and Isle of Wight Surrey West Sussex

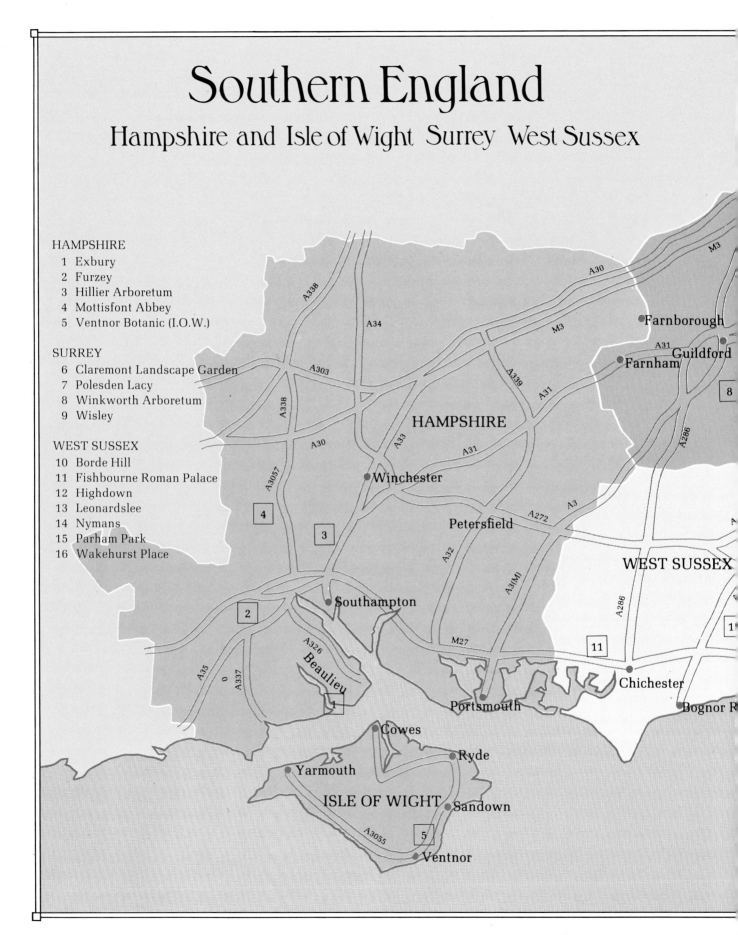

HAMPSHIRE
  1 Exbury
  2 Furzey
  3 Hillier Arboretum
  4 Mottisfont Abbey
  5 Ventnor Botanic (I.O.W.)

SURREY
  6 Claremont Landscape Garden
  7 Polesden Lacy
  8 Winkworth Arboretum
  9 Wisley

WEST SUSSEX
  10 Borde Hill
  11 Fishbourne Roman Palace
  12 Highdown
  13 Leonardslee
  14 Nymans
  15 Parham Park
  16 Wakehurst Place

HAMPSHIRE

WEST SUSSEX

Farnborough

Guildford
Farnham

8

A30

M3

M3

A31

A339

A338

A34

A303

A338

A30

A31

A3

A272

A31(M)

A32

A286

A3057

Winchester

Petersfield

Southampton

M27

A35

A337

A326

Beaulieu

Portsmouth

Chichester

Bognor R

11

Cowes

Ryde

Yarmouth

ISLE OF WIGHT

Sandown

A3055

Ventnor

4

3

2

1

11

5

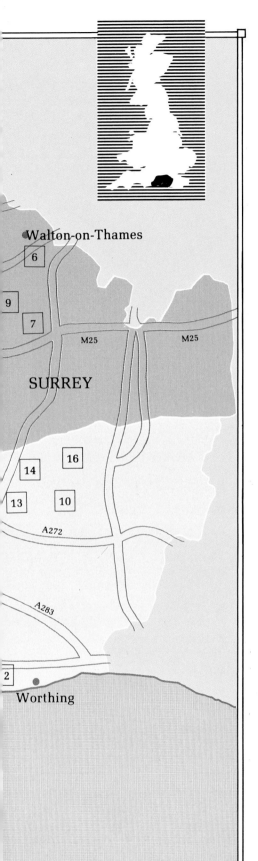

Walton-on-Thames

6

9

7

M25   M25

SURREY

16

14

13   10

A272

A283

2

Worthing

HAMPSHIRE

· 1 ·
EXBURY
nr Southampton

This 80-hectare (200-acre) woodland garden, with its complex pattern of walks, is so vast that ideally several visits are needed to take in its many delights. Spring and early summer is the only time to see it, however, for despite its very fine oaks and conifers, Exbury is chiefly renowned for the Rothschild collection of rhododendrons and azaleas. This is the most comprehensive array of rhododendrons in Britain, which includes extremely rare species from the Himalayas, China, Tibet and Sri Lanka, as well as new hybrids raised here, such as the exquisite apricot-coloured "Lady Chamberlain". The Exbury strain of azaleas, with large, strongly scented flowers, is also world-famous. The camellias, too, are very fine.

Garden open March to July, daily.

Exbury. woodland garden.

· 2 ·
FURZEY
Minstead, nr Lyndhurst

This lovely plantsman's garden, laid out around a low thatched cottage, contains an immense variety of plants, including many exotic species, principally in large island beds which are interspersed by lawns and grass paths. In front of the cottage is a large area devoted to heathers, and some of the shrubs, such as eucryphias, embothriums and rhododendrons, are of enormous dimensions. Ground cover plants provide continuous colour in spring, and the combination throughout of native and rarer imported species give Furzey its special fascination.

Open all year, daily.

· 3 ·
HILLIER ARBORETUM
Ampfield, nr Romsey

The nursery firm of Hillier and Sons acquired this site in the 1950s, originally with a view to propagating conifers, camellias and other species. Since then it has been greatly expanded to create a collection of trees and shrubs, the largest of its kind in Britain which, in addition to being botanically important, is tastefully planted in a beautifully landscaped setting around Jermyns House. There are

areas for especially rare and tender plants, a fine collection of heathers across Jermyns Lane, and splendid borders of herbaceous perennials and roses. The size and variety of this ornamental collection warrants a succession of seasonal visits.

Open all year Mon. to Fri., also Sat., Sun. afternoons March to early Nov.

· 4 ·
MOTTISFONT ABBEY
Mottisfont, nr Romsey

The Georgian house, built on the site of a medieval monastery, stands on the banks of the River Test. On and around the broad lawns are many tall specimen trees including a giant plane, beeches, oaks, sweet chestnuts, blue Atlas cedars, etc. The garden, developed since 1957 by the National Trust, has a fine avenue of pleached limes, carpeted with spring flowers, designed by Geoffrey Jellicoe, and a beautiful walled rose garden planned and planted by Graham Thomas. In addition to a splendid collection of shrub roses, there are herbaceous borders which blend delightfully with the roses in the beds and on the walls. The spring which is now channelled to the river below the house is the original "font" which determined the site and gave the abbey its name.

Garden open April to Sept., Sun. to Thurs. NT

· 5 ·
VENTNOR BOTANIC GARDEN
Ventnor, Isle of Wight

Thanks to its extreme southerly situation on a cliff edge which is well protected from all sides, this fine municipal garden, which dates only from 1970, is becoming known for its interesting collection of exotic shrubs. Unusual conifers are growing in the pinetum and other woodland areas, a rose garden is set around a large pool, and other specialized sections include a palm garden and a rock garden. For visitors not botanically minded, there are various amusements, including a museum of smuggling.

Open all year, daily.

SURREY

· 6 ·
CLAREMONT LANDSCAPE GARDEN
Esher

The garden of this 18th-century house was begun before 1720 by Vanbrugh and Bridgeman and subsequently extended and transformed by Kent and Brown. It is the oldest surviving landscape garden in England, recently restored by the National Trust, which acquired it in 1949. Original features include the lake and surrounding woodland, with a temple and a belvedere by Vanbrugh, and among the reconstructed areas is an avenue of limes, an island with a pavilion, a grotto and a large turf amphitheatre. There are many impressive trees,

since 1944 have been maintained by the National Trust. They are designed, in the manner characteristic of the early years of the present century, as a series of distinct but inter-connected areas, some enclosed by hedges, others left open. The attraction of these gardens, each self-contained and individual, yet harmonizing well with those adjoining, is enhanced by the ornamentation chosen by Mrs Greville, including griffins on the terraces and sundials, seats, urns, vases and statuary at different focal points. A yew hedge with marble statues against it forms a background to a small plot of grass close to the house where Mrs Greville is buried.

The enclosures on either side of the central path include a large rose garden of considerable variety, despite the fact that the chalky soil is not ideal for roses, an iris garden packed with species popular in the early part of this century, and a variegated lavender garden which gives off a powerful scent in summer. Beyond these enclosed gardens, along a wall, is a four-sectioned herbaceous border. A steep bank, planted with shrubs and notable for a mass of the short, spreading *Juniperus media* "Pfitzerana", leads down to the main lawn with splendid trees that include beeches, spruces and maples. The lawns, gardens and woodland areas cover in all some 12 hectares (30 acres).

Garden open all year, daily. NT

including cedars of Lebanon, oaks, beeches, yews and hollies.

Open all year, daily. NT

· 7 ·

POLESDEN LACEY
nr Dorking

The neo-classical Regency house is perched on a chalk ridge overlooking the Surrey countryside, surrounded by broad lawns and clusters of trees. It was once owned by the playwright Richard Brinsley Sheridan, who probably extended the long grass walk that bears his name. This is guarded by two slender stone pillars and decorated with urns and other ornaments, with a Doric portico at the far end. Soon after Sheridan's death the original house was pulled down to be replaced by the present one. The formal gardens which visitors see today were laid out by Cheal and Sons for Mrs Ronald Greville who bought the property in 1906, and

· 8 ·

WINKWORTH ARBORETUM
Hascombe, nr Godalming

The arboretum, created by Dr Wilfred Fox and given to the National Trust in 1952, now covers about 40 hectares (100 acres). It is beautifully situated in a sheltered hillside position overlooking a lake, and contains a magnificent collection of mainly broad-leaved trees as well as azaleas, rhododendrons and magnolias. The trees were planted especially for autumn colour and one of

·9·
Wisley Garden

nr Ripley, Surrey

The world-famous gardens at Wisley, owned and maintained by the Royal Horticultural Society, exhibit every form of gardening, both practical and ornamental, and are, apart from their obvious attraction as a showplace, an important centre for education and scientific research, containing laboratories, extensive greenhouses, model gardens catering for all possible needs, and areas specially reserved for trials of new plant species. Much of the research goes on behind the scenes, but everything is conducted in a setting of extreme beauty and natural variety.

The derelict estate was purchased in 1878 by G.F. Wilson, an amateur gardener, who developed a six-acre woodland garden, which is still at the heart of the much bigger garden area developed since 1904 by the Royal Horticultural Society.

From the main entrance visitors can make a circular tour of the gardens, passing the laboratory building with its terraced lawns. The grassy Broad Walk, flanked by two long, spectacular mixed borders, leads to a demonstration

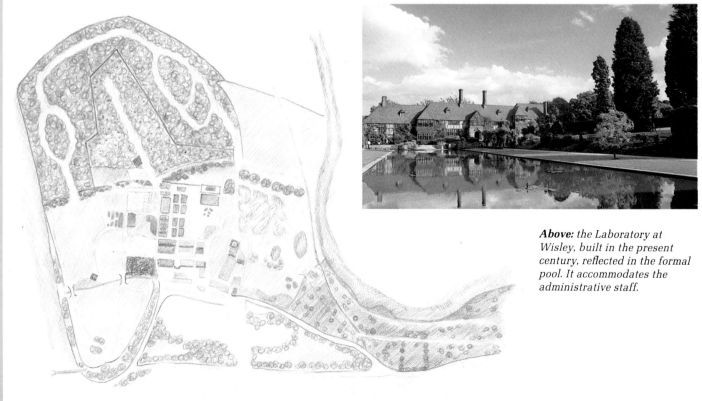

Above: *the Laboratory at Wisley, built in the present century, reflected in the formal pool. It accommodates the administrative staff.*

Left and below: although Wisley is primarily important as a research and training establishment, its wide-ranging display of ornamental plants provides interest and enjoyment for innumerable visitors at all seasons.

area comprising gardens that specialize in herbaceous plants, shrubs, bulbs and annuals, and new varieties of shrub and climbing roses.

The path now runs uphill through the informally planted woodland area of Battleston Hill, with magnificent banks of rhododendrons, azaleas, magnolias, camellias and other shade-loving plants. Beyond are greenhouses containing exotic tropical species, cacti and orchids, and then the area devoted to fruits, mainly apples, pears and plums, but also soft fruits. The nearby model gardens include one for disabled people, and the herb garden contains both culinary and medicinal species.

The walk continues past the main rose borders into the Alpine meadow, with scattered outcrops of rock, at its best in spring when it is bright with dwarf daffodils. Adjoining the meadow is the marvellous rock garden, dating from 1911, although since enlarged and modified. A path zigzags up and down among a wide variety of alpine plants, and streams and waterfalls culminate at the foot of the garden in a pond bordered by aquatic perennials.

G.F. Wilson's wild garden is the oldest part of Wisley, with hybrid rhododendrons, blue Himalayan poppies, primulas, lilies and many other woodland species. Beyond is the park-like Seven Acres, containing a superb heather garden and a lake with an island in the centre.

The pinetum, to the north, dates from the early part of the present century and contains a good range of conifers; and beyond this is Howard's Field, where an interesting miscellany of plants flourish on very dry, sandy soil.

Visitors now return to the house, in front of which are the walled and formal gardens. The latter were designed by Lanning Roper and Geoffrey Jellicoe, replacing the old greenhouses which formerly stood here. The central feature is a large, formal canal with a multiple-jet fountain. On the site of an old potting shed an open loggia leads to the walled garden with two parterres, one used for spring and summer bedding plants, the other for roses, small shrubs and perennials.

Gardens open all year, daily.

Dr Fox's original contributions was a drift of Japanese maples in the section known as The Bowl. Among the other species notable for their superb foliage tints are sorbus, rhus, liquidambar, sweet gums and scarlet oaks. At one point there is a long flight of 93 steps. The woodland paths provide endless fascination and the lakeside walks offer good views of the surrounding countryside.

Arboretum open all year, daily. NT

· 9 ·
WISLEY GARDEN
nr Ripley

Special feature – see page 30.

WEST SUSSEX

· 10 ·
BORDE HILL
Haywards Heath

The charming stone manor stands in a lovely parkland and woodland setting, and the garden is notable for its trees and shrubs, including a wonderful collection of rhododendrons and azaleas. The south lawn, with its ha-ha, has fine views of the South Downs, and there are formal areas near the house including a terrace garden. Most of the ground, however, consists of woodland with informal planting. Colonel Stevenson Clarke, who began his new planting here in 1893, was a keen collector, raising many species from seed. His rhododendrons increased so rapidly as to spill over into the surrounding woods, and they are especially impressive in one of the two woodland dells, the second of which is a water and bog garden, with splendid examples of the ostrich plume and other ferns. There is also a pinetum with excellent conifers, while other trees, including maples, are scattered all over the garden.

Garden open March and Oct., Sat., Sun.; April to Sept., daily.

· 11 ·
FISHBOURNE ROMAN PALACE
Fishbourne, nr Chichester

When the site of a Roman military headquarters was recently discovered at Fishbourne, the outlines of a garden were traced, including the better quality soil imported for growing various plants. A model gives an idea of what the residential buildings and garden looked like, and on part of the available site a simple, symmetrical garden, with a courtyard, terrace, lawns, box hedges and herbs, has been reconstructed. It is a uniquely fascinating example of the earliest form of garden made in Britain.

Open March to Nov., daily.

· 12 ·
HIGHDOWN
nr Worthing

Sir Frederick Stern made this garden in a disused chalk quarry in 1909. Anthony Waterer, the nurseryman, predicted that nothing would grow there, but today the garden has achieved international fame. Around the quarry a profusion of plants grows, to all appearance, naturally, in an attractive grass and water setting. The spring displays, especially of anemones, crocuses, daffodils and cyclamens, are particularly beautiful, and there are many interesting trees. On the slopes of the down peonies, irises and even lilies do surprisingly well in the relatively thin soil over solid chalk. It is a delightful place and the views are marvellous.

Open April to Sept., daily; Oct. to March, weekdays.

· 13 ·
LEONARDSLEE
Lower Beeding, Horsham

This is one of the greatest woodland gardens in Britain, comparable to Windsor's Valley Gardens, owned, created and maintained by one of the most distinguished names in gardening, the Loder family. It covers more than 40 hectares (100 acres) on a hillside that slopes down to a valley with several hammer ponds, so named because they were man-made for powering the hammers of old ironworks. Sir Edmund Loder, who in addition to his other pursuits (including athletics and big-game hunting) was a dedicated botanist, began planting the garden in 1888, not aiming for conventional Victorian formality but resolved to exploit to the full the natural possibilities of this exceptionally favoured site. His particular favourites were rhododendrons and it is principally for these that Leonardslee is famous. As well as collecting existing species, he set out to raise new ones, and over the years many hybrids have been created, but none more renowned than Sir Edmund's own *Rhododendron loderi*, a cross between *R. griffithianum* and *R. fortunei*. These sweetly scented plants have by now grown to tree-like proportions and still hold pride of place among innumerable others.

Although the rhododendrons and azaleas create the most spectacular banks of colour, there are also splendid magnolias, flowering cherries and camellias, these last being grown both in the open and in greenhouses. Banksian roses adorn the walls of the house and palms grow in such profusion that they have had to be thinned out. There are fine oaks and maples, and a wide range of conifers, including dwarf species. Among the taller specimens are redwoods and wellingtonias, Japanese birch and many other rarities. The entire garden, with its meandering paths, is a delight, especially in spring and early summer, and again when the autumn foliage tints are breathtaking.

Gardens open mid-May to mid-June, daily, then to Oct., Sat. and Sun.

· 14 ·
NYMANS
Handcross

Special feature – see page 34.

· 15 ·
PARHAM PARK
Pulborough

This magnificent Elizabethan mansion, which was built by Sir Thomas Palmer, who sailed with Drake to Cadiz, has 2.8 hectares (7 acres) of pleasure grounds in 18th-century style, with a lake, statuary and fine trees. A 1.6-hectare (4-acre) walled garden with herbaceous borders, redesigned by Peter Coats, is the main attraction.

Open April to Sept., Sun., Wed., Thurs.

·16·

WAKEHURST PLACE
Ardingly

The tree and shrub collection at Wakehurst Place is, in some respects, even more remarkable than that of the Royal Botanic Gardens, Kew, to which it forms an annexe. Thanks to a favoured situation high on a ridge between two valleys, which provides protection against late winter frosts, and by reason of its acid soil, the garden accommodates a wide range of tender and rare plant species.

The landscaped gardens, with their magnificent trees, extending past a lake and into woodland, were developed at the turn of the present century by the then owners of the Elizabethan house, Sir Thomas and Lady Boord; they created the rock garden beside the pond and initiated the famous rhododendron collection with seeds imported from Asia. Gerald Loder, later Lord Wakehurst, then brought together the incomparable collection of plants, many from the southern hemisphere, that adorn the garden today.

Rhododendrons are everywhere at Wakehurst in a dazzling array of white, pink, yellow, crimson, scarlet and purple; so, too, in due season, are azaleas, magnolias and maples. Lord Wakehurst's Heath Garden is especially fine, with many additions to the original heathers, and the flower beds and borders glow with colour through-out the growing season. The garden's chief glory, however, is its assembly of trees, both coniferous and broadleaved, in the pinetum, and in the extensive woodland areas beyond. Notable specimens include a *Magnolia campbellii,* a Handkerchief Tree, *Davidia involucrata,* the Mexican Pine, *Pinus patula,* the Himalaya Larch, *Larix griffithiana* and the rare Chinese conifer, *Keteleeria davidiana.*

Short or long walks can be taken from the house, the former taking in the walled, heath, rock and water gardens, and the attractive shrub borders, the latter including the Westwood Valley and Lake, the Horsebridge Woods, Bloomer's Valley and Bethlehem Wood, back to the starting point.

Gardens open all year, daily.

Wakehurst Place.

·14·
Nymans

Handcross, West Sussex

Situated about 120m (400ft) above sea-level and sheltered by the tall trees of St Leonard's forest, the gardens at Nymans constitute a delightful blend of formality and informality. Ludwig Messel, owner of the house, began to lay them out a century ago, and the influence of his two friends, Gertrude Jekyll and William Robinson, is strongly apparent in certain parts. The fertile, sandy loam proved ideal for a wide variety of trees and flowering shrubs, including the splendid rhododendrons, magnolias and camellias for which the gardens are most famous. The work of expansion was continued by Ludwig's son, Colonel Leonard Messel, and subsequent generations of the family, and by the National Trust, which acquired the property in 1954.

Despite its size and proximity to a main road, Nymans is an intimate and peaceful spot. The gardens lie on either side of the grey stone skeleton of the original house which was largely destroyed by fire in 1947.

Visitors enter at the western end of the garden, passing the pinetum with its little classical temple. Oaks and sweet chestnuts mingle with pines, cypresses, cedars and junipers, while banks of shrubs include large-leaved rhododendrons, hydrangeas and the renowned "Nymansay" hybrid eucryphias with glossy evergreen leaves and handsome white flowers with golden anthers in late summer. In one direction is a lime avenue leading to a balustraded prospect over park and woodland; in the other a path runs through the top garden (originally an overflow for the masses of plants imported, mainly from the southern hemisphere, in the 1920s and 1930s when the gardens were expanded), and the rose garden, into the formal walled garden. This is roughly oval in shape, with two paths crossing at right angles and dividing the garden into four segments, each of different character. One path is especially colourful in spring, the other in summer, edged as it is with two long herbaceous borders partly designed by William Robinson. At the very centre is an Italian fountain guarded by four clipped yews with crown-like domes.

On the other side of the house is a broad sweep of lawn with specimen trees and banks of flowering shrubs. The house walls are mantled with climbers such as roses, clematis, wis-

The classical temple.

Far left: *the Byzantine urn in the Sunk Garden.*
Left: *the dovecote, made of the same grey stone as used for the house walls.*

Far left: *part of the skeleton of the original house, destroyed by fire.*
Left: *the herbaceous borders and fountain, with four topiary trees.*

teria and jasmine, and the terraces are massed with summer-flowering plants. There is attractive yew and box topiary work, and a delightful stone dovecote with a conical roof. Particularly remarkable are the camellias, many of them hybrids raised here and bearing Messel family names, constituting one of the finest collections in the country. A circular sunken garden with formal flower beds has a Byzantine urn as centrepiece and an Italian stone loggia. This was laid out as part of Ludwig Messel's original design, as were the nearby rock and heather gardens, and the Japanese garden with stone pergola in the south-east corner.

Across the main road is an extensive woodland area planted with rhododendrons, and a wild garden containing many unusual plants from Asia, and a section called Tasmania with plant species from that island.

Nymans is a wonderful place at any season and visitors can obtain information on special spring, summer and autumn walks.

Gardens open April to Oct., daily except Mon., Fri. NT

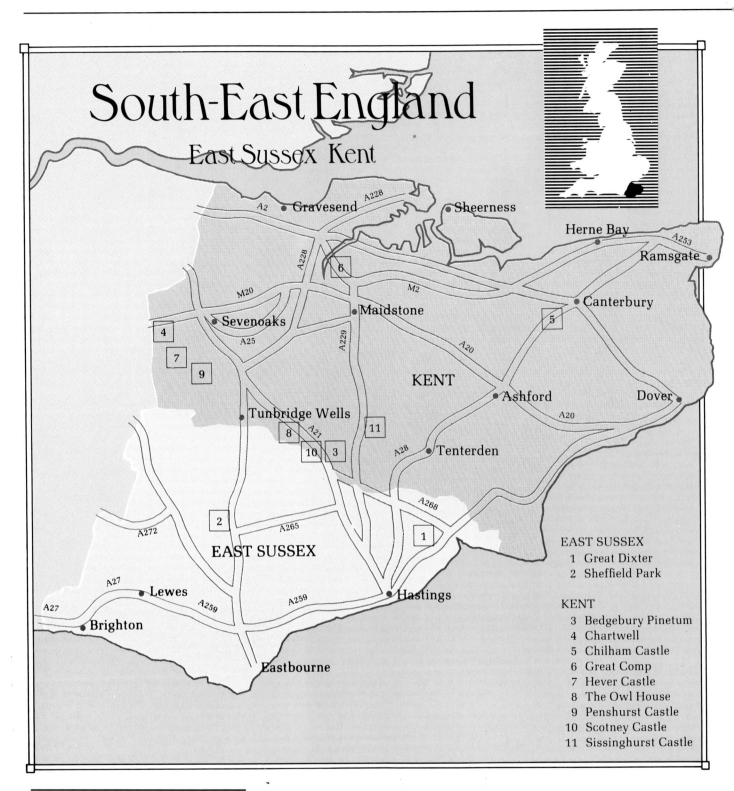

South-East England
East Sussex Kent

A2	Gravesend
A228	Sheerness
	Herne Bay
A253	Ramsgate
A228	6
M20	
M2	Canterbury
Sevenoaks	Maidstone
A25	5
4	A229
7	KENT
9	A20
Tunbridge Wells	Ashford
8	A20
A21	Dover
10	3	11
A28	Tenterden
A268	
2	1
A272	A265
EAST SUSSEX	
A27	Lewes
A259	A259
Brighton	Hastings
Eastbourne	

EAST SUSSEX
1 Great Dixter
2 Sheffield Park

KENT
3 Bedgebury Pinetum
4 Chartwell
5 Chilham Castle
6 Great Comp
7 Hever Castle
8 The Owl House
9 Penshurst Castle
10 Scotney Castle
11 Sissinghurst Castle

EAST SUSSEX

·1·

GREAT DIXTER
Northiam

The house was enlarged early in the present century by Edwin Lutyens, who also designed parts of the garden. Gertrude Jekyll advised on the planting but never worked here; her influence is evident in the pattern of separate "rooms" which accommodate a wonderful variety of annual and hardy perennial plants and shrubs, reflecting the tastes and skills of the Lloyd family who own it. The front lawn with its yew hedges has been maintained as a flowering meadow. The sunken garden is planted on three sides, with a central lily pond. The famous long border combines herbaceous flowers and shrubs which give continuous colour from spring to autumn.

Garden open April to mid-Oct., Tues. to Sun.

· 2 ·
SHEFFIELD PARK
Uckfield

James Wyatt, First Lord Sheffield, called in "Capability" Brown to landscape the garden of his house around 1775. Although no record of his work survives, Brown probably designed the two lower lakes in the shallow valley south-east of the house, laid out the stretch of lawn sweeping up to the house walls, and framed it all with the belts and clumps of trees so characteristic of his manner. Humphry Repton was also invited to improve the design but nothing is known of his contribution. Over a century later two more lakes were added by James Pulham for the Third Earl, fed by water pumped up into a reservoir. The slope between these two lakes was filled with rocks, over which flowed a connecting stream and cascade. The third phase occurred in the present century after Arthur Soames acquired the property in 1909. During the next 25 years he completely transformed the garden, extending the top lakes, building a cataract between the two, and planted a richly varied collection of broad-leaved trees, conifers and shrubs.

The result is the magnificent woodland spectacle that makes Sheffield Park, now owned by the National Trust, one of the finest gardens of its

Below: *Great Dixter.*
Bottom: *Sheffield Park.*

kind. The conditions are ideal, with a perfect setting, good acidic soil and a favourable microclimate. In the woods there are rhododendrons, azaleas and many other flowering shrubs for spring and summer colour. Hybrids raised here include the cross between *Rhododendron discolor* and *R. griffithianum*, known as the "Angelo" group, and there are examples, among others, of the famous Leonardslee *R. loderi* large-flowered hybrids.

For many visitors the chief glory of Sheffield Park is the blaze of red and gold autumn colour, provided by maples, beeches, taxodiums and particularly the masses of North American tupelos, *Nyssa sylvatica*. The conifers, too, are remarkable, including Lawson cypresses, redwoods, umbrella pines, junipers, cedars, larches and many more.

Garden open end-March to Nov., daily except Mon. NT

KENT

· 3 ·
BEDGEBURY PINETUM
Goudhurst

In 1924 the Royal Botanic Gardens, Kew, and the Forestry Commission acquired this 40-hectare (100-acre) estate specifically for conifers which did not grow well at Kew. Now managed by the Forestry Commission alone, the pinetum contains one of the biggest and most varied collection of its kind in Europe. Individual sections include a spruce valley, a cypress valley and a sequoia grove, but this does not begin to suggest the enormous profusion of trees that flourish here, not only several hundreds of species of conifers but also maples, oaks, birches, southern beeches and liquidambars. The pinetum is beautifully landscaped with streams flowing through two valleys into a large hammer lake.

Open all year, daily.

· 4 ·
CHARTWELL
Westerham

The former home of Sir Winston Churchill, now owned by the National Trust, stands on top of a small ridge, and the lovely garden commands a panoramic view of the countryside. There are many reminders of the former owner, including the lakes with the black swans he painted, his studio, the wall he himself built around what is now a marvellous rose garden, and the path flanked by borders of yellow roses planted to commemorate Sir Winston and Lady Churchill's golden wedding. A pavilion in the grounds is known as the Marlborough Pavilion. The garden proper is around the house, and the terraces, steps, interlinked enclosures, walls and pergolas are planted with a rich variety of flowers and shrubs. The informal areas, with pools and waterfalls, are also delightful.

Garden open April to Oct., daily except Mon., Fri. NT

· 5 ·
CHILHAM CASTLE
nr Canterbury

This Jacobean house stands on the site of an ancient Roman fort. The gardens, consisting of an extensive landscaped park, formal terracing, rose and rock gardens, etc., reflect the changing styles of more than three centuries, and may originally have been laid out in the 1630s by Charles I's gardener, the elder John Tradescant. Certainly the formal terraces date from earlier than 1777 or thereabouts when "Capability" Brown (who is recorded as having spent only a few days at Chilham to tender general advice) laid out the park with its lakes and trees.

The series of descending grass terraces, connected by a flight of brick steps, are lined with flower borders and each level is backed by a wall with many varieties of climbers. The house walls also provide background colour with wisteria, Banksian roses, pyracantha, etc. The three terraces are further adorned with immense topiary yew

specimens, and at the edge of the large lawn below are 10 smaller yews shaped like chess pieces. A low wall or ha-ha forms the boundary between the lawn and the park.

All around the house are many remarkable trees, some of them undoubtedly dating from about the time the castle was built. On the top terrace there is a gigantic holm oak, its trunks bound together by chains, and a Judas tree. Others include an ancient mulberry, a tulip tree, and numerous cedars. Near the main gate is a lime avenue and there is another avenue, over 1.6km (1 mile) in length, of Spanish chestnuts.

Various forms of summer entertainments at Chilham Castle include medieval jousting and displays of falconry.

Gardens open mid-March to Oct., daily.

· 6 ·
GREAT COMP
Borough Green, nr Sevenoaks

The lovely garden of this 17th-century house, designed and laid out since 1958 by the former owners, is situated some 110m (360ft) above sea level on a gentle slope, well sheltered by conifers and broad-leaved trees. Within the framework of such trees irregular blocks and drifts of shrubs have been planted, and a continuous policy of soil improvement has fostered the growth of many interesting and unusual species. There are splendid rhododendrons, azaleas and magnolias, heathers and herbaceous plants, and a bog garden.

Open April to Oct., daily.

· 7 ·
HEVER CASTLE
Hever

Special feature – see page 40.

· 8 ·
THE OWL HOUSE
Lamberhurst

This fairly new 5-hectare (13-acre) garden surrounds a 16th-century cottage once used by "owlers" or

smugglers, and the owl motif occurs frequently, on the entrance gate pillars and on the terraces. Near the house there are neat paths, flower borders, rose-clad pergolas and a pool, with scented climbers on the walls. Away from the house roses grow more freely, some trained on tripods in a meadow. And beyond the lawn is the woodland area, with fine oaks and birches, and masses of rhododendrons, azaleas and other flowering shrubs.

Open all year, daily.

· 9 ·
PENSHURST PLACE
Penshurst

The lovely medieval manor house, with later additions, is set in a beautiful 4-hectare (10-acre) walled garden of much more recent design but in the formal 17th-century style, with terrace, parterre, paths, flower borders and hedged enclosures. In front of the house is the Italian garden, a large, rectangular parterre with raised terraces and large beds, some with red roses and outlined in box, others entirely of clipped box shaped into low slabs. There is a circular lily basin with a fountain topped by a bronze statue of a youth. There are splendid borders, throughout and the individual areas include a rose garden, nut garden, kitchen garden and magnolia garden. A long yew alley opens into the walled pool known as Diana's Bath. The garden also contains numerous fruit trees.

Garden open April to Sept., daily except Mon.

· 10 ·
SCOTNEY CASTLE
Lamberhurst

The setting for the garden of Scotney Castle is undoubtedly one of the most picturesque and dramatic in the British Isles; a small lake, surrounded by trees, with a ruined castle in the centre. This is the focal point for a beautiful 19th-century landscape garden created by the Hussey family and, in recent years, maintained with the help of the National Trust.

The original castle, a fortified house

·7·
Hever Castle

Hever, Kent

The moated castle, converted into a comfortable Tudor manor house, was the birthplace and home of Henry VIII's second wife Anne Boleyn, and there is a path and garden bearing her name. After her disgrace and execution the family fortunes declined and it was not until 1903 that they were restored by the immensely wealthy American William Astor, later First Viscount Astor of Hever. He built a Tudor-style "village" behind the renovated house to accommodate his guests and staff and proceeded to lay out new gardens all around. It was a colossally ambitious scheme which involved draining the entire site, diverting the River Eden to create an ornamental lake complete with rocks and cascade, bringing in fully-grown trees from Ashdown Forest, excavating an outer moat, and commissioning the landscaping specialists Joseph Cheal and Sons to plant the avenues and make a series of formal gardens between the two moats.

To the east of the castle, the walls of which are bright with climbing roses, clematis, wisteria and jasmine, is Anne Boleyn's Garden, which includes a maze with yews imported from Holland, a small herb garden containing many culinary and aromatic species, and a

Silver Garden, planted in silver and grey, to commemorate the silver wedding anniversary of the present Lord and Lady Astor. Another small garden contains topiary Tudor-style chessmen in yew. The gardens are surrounded by pergolas with decorative climbing plants and there is additional colour from the water lilies in the moats.

The most spectacular and unusual feature of Hever is Viscount Astor's Italian Garden, situated outside the formal moated gardens and facing the lake. This was designed to accommodate a collection of classical statues and sculptures which he had previously accumulated when American Ambassador in Rome. There are roses, pergolas, pools and grottos here, but the principal and most arresting feature is the long flower-clad wall with bays in which are placed statues, busts, columns, urns, sarcophagi and other classical objects. The broad walk with this astonishing display of antiquities, beautifully framed with herbaceous and climbing plants, leads to a colonnaded loggia with a marble fountain, with views over the lake. Adjoining the Italian Garden is an interesting rock garden made of sandstone slabs and planted mainly with blue-flowering shrubs, and the rose garden.

Away from the formal areas there are other features to enjoy. On one side of the lake, and running across it, is the Chestnut Avenue. There is a lovely Rhododendron Walk and, on the other shore of the lake, Anne Boleyn's Walk, with mature specimen trees, access to which is from the so-called Golden Stairs. And for those who are sufficiently energetic there is an enjoyable walk right around the lake.

Garden open April to Oct., daily.

*Viscount Astor filled his Italian Garden at Hever with classical statuary and carvings collected while he was ambassador in Rome. The pictures on this page and **below left** show glimpses of the garden.*

Top left: *the lake in the grounds of Hever Castle.*
Far left: *the entrance to the Rose Garden.*

rather than a stronghold proper, dated from the 14th century. The house acquired by the Hussey family, however, in 1778 was a 17th-century villa alongside the round tower of the old castle. In 1835 Edward Hussey decided to pull the existing house down, as being too damp to live in, replacing it with a new country house near by on higher ground. It was built for him in neo-Tudor style by Anthony Salvin, using ironstone from the quarry in the existing garden. Strongly influenced by the picturesque school of writers and gardeners, Edward Hussey resolved to create a garden of romantic character, demolishing all but the round tower of the castle and deliberately making of it a ruin to form the centrepiece of the landscape garden on the surrounding slopes. Shrubs and trees, including splendid North American conifers, were planted, and the quarry itself converted into a rock garden. The balustraded bastion high above the quarry today provides the best view down the wooded slope to the moated castle ruin far below, and the walk from the upper lawn through the shrub garden to the lake is delightful at any season. Beyond the castle, in a meadow on the far side, is a great cedar of Lebanon, and other dominant specimens include cypresses, incense cedars and redwoods. Rhododendrons and azaleas are followed by pink calico flowers *(Kalmia latifolia)* and buddleias, and the waterside species include masses of royal fern *(Osmunda regalis)*. The walls of the old castle are bright in summer with rambler roses.

Garden open end March to mid-Nov., daily except Mon., Tues. NT

Scotney Castle.

·11·
SISSINGHURST CASTLE
Sissinghurst

The famous garden created from 1930 onwards by Vita Sackville-West and her husband Sir Harold Nicolson has much in common with that of Hidcote Manor, and both have had a powerful influence on subsequent garden design. A medieval moated manor belonging to the de Saxenhurst family once stood on the site but the dilapidated house bought by the Nicolsons, dominated by its twin-turreted tower, dated from the reign of Henry VIII. Around what remained of the house, including the courtyard and scattered outbuildings, these two dedicated gardeners created their masterpiece, a combination, as Vita Sackville-West described it, of "maximum formality of design with maximum informality of planting".

Although the garden at Sissinghurst, like that of Hidcote, is laid out on the principle of a series of interlinked outdoor "rooms", each with its distinctive character, visitors are invariably struck not by the intricacy of pattern but by the sheer luxuriance of variety and colour in a cottage-garden atmosphere.

Sissinghurst, now owned by the National Trust, is especially renowned for its marvellous collection of old-fashioned and shrub roses, and the rose garden is rightly one of the main attractions. In its centre is one of two rondels, a grassy circle of clipped yew, the name being derived from the circular hedged enclosure where hops were once dried. The cottage garden is another popular area, usually planted in bright shades of red, orange and yellow, with a copper container in the centre. The white garden, particularly spectacular in June, resembles a miniature parterre with the different sections given over principally to white and grey plants. The charming herb garden in the south corner has a central flat marble vase supported by lions, and leads to the nuttery, originally a plantation of Kentish cob-nuts but underplanted by Vita Sackville-West with masses of polyanthus, which later had to be replaced by mixed perennials. At the end of this is the lime walk, very lovely in spring. Among other attractions are the long yew walk and the orchard adjoining the old moat.

Garden open April to Oct., daily. NT

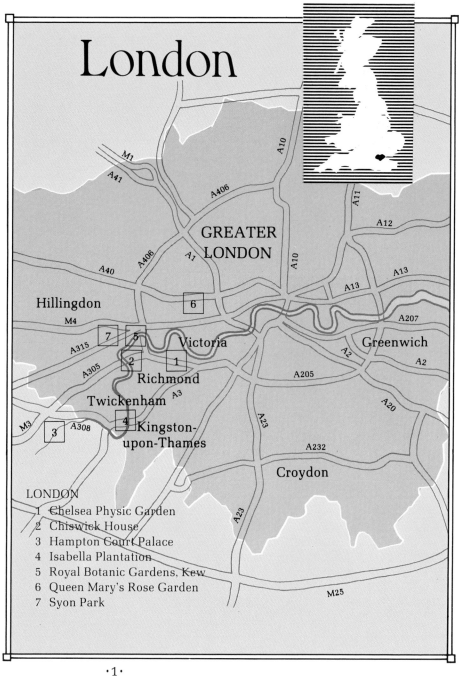

London

GREATER LONDON

Hillingdon

Victoria

Greenwich

Richmond

Twickenham

Kingston-
upon-Thames

Croydon

LONDON
1 Chelsea Physic Garden
2 Chiswick House
3 Hampton Court Palace
4 Isabella Plantation
5 Royal Botanic Gardens, Kew
6 Queen Mary's Rose Garden
7 Syon Park

Chelsea Physic Garden.

·1·
CHELSEA PHYSIC GARDEN
Chelsea

Founded in 1673 by the Society of Apothecaries, this is Britain's second oldest botanical garden. For three centuries only botanical, medical and art students were permitted entrance but today the thousands of interesting horticultural species can be studied and enjoyed by the public at large. The garden has always been maintained by charitable donations and thanks to money currently being raised by public appeal its immediate future seems assured.

Open mid-April to mid-Oct., Wed., Sun.

·2·
CHISWICK HOUSE
Chiswick

After returning from a "Grand Tour" in Europe, the Earl of Burlington drew up his own designs for the villa at Chiswick which was built for him from 1725-9. Having been particularly impressed by the work of the 16th-century Italian architect Andrea Palladio, and particularly Palladio's Villa Rotonda near Vicenza, Lord Burlington

elected to build his two-storey villa in similar style, setting it in a garden which reflected his classical tastes. He had, in fact, begun to lay out the garden even before building the house, in fairly formal manner, with radiating avenues and temples, but called in his friend, the architect and artist William Kent, to transform it in the early 1730s. Kent himself was strongly influenced by Italian culture, having lived in Italy for eight years, and proceeded to remodel the existing garden, accentuating the neo-classical features but giving it a more naturalistic appearance. Not much remains of this garden, although it has been well restored, conveying something of the original atmosphere, with its blend of formality and informality.

Many of Kent's modifications were inspired by Renaissance gardens in Italy, as, for example, the elaborate grotto and cascade, and the spectacular exedra, a semi-circular area within a yew hedge, against which Kent placed urns, sphinxes and statues, including three representing Caesar, Pompey and Cicero, said to have come from Hadrian's villa at Tivoli. Kent also converted Charles Bridgeman's artificial canal into what appears to be a meandering river.

The conservatory, with its fine

·3·
Hampton Court Palace

East Molesey

Cardinal Wolsey began to build his great mansion on the bank of the River Thames in 1514, providing it with a garden which contained sheltered walks, knots and fountains. In 1529, under strong pressure, he handed Hampton Court over as a gift to his royal master Henry VIII. The king enlarged the palace, which became his favourite residence, and altered the garden. Pictures and written records show that in addition to providing himself with bowling greens, a tennis court and a tiltyard, he planted a rose garden, erected a huge mount on a foundation of thousands of bricks, with a summerhouse on the top, and laid out an elaborate parterre of flower beds. This was surrounded by tall poles painted in the royal colours, which were surmounted by brightly coloured carvings of heraldic animals, the "King's Beastes".

Despite the names given to parts of the modern gardens (Tudor Garden and Henry VIII's Sunken Garden), no vestige of these original Tudor designs survives. Some modifications were made under the Stuart kings, notably the construction of an artificial watercourse to bring water to the garden from the River Colne eight miles away (the level of the adjoining Thames being too low at that point), but radical changes only began to occur at the end of the 17th century, giving the garden much of its present appearance.

William III and Mary commissioned Sir Christopher Wren to transform the Tudor palace and employed the nurserymen London and Wise to redesign the garden in the then-fashionable French manner. The formal areas were certainly more elaborate, as originally conceived, with a greater number of fountains, parterres and decorative features; but the existing Great Fountain Garden and Privy Garden faithfully reflect those innovations. The Fountain Garden, with its radiating avenues, lies below the east front of the palace, and remains a masterpiece. On the south side is the Privy Garden, with raised ground on either side, one comprising an alley of wych elms known as Queen Mary's Bower, leading through a gate to the walled Tudor Garden area. The Long Walk and Broad Walk were laid out, the great canal pool or Long Water was given its definite shape, clipped trees and shrubs were planted, statues were set up and two Frenchmen, Daniel Marot and Jean Tijou, called in to advise on various points of garden design, drew up the plans for twelve wrought-iron screens, which can still be admired both in the Great Fountain and Privy Gardens.

The famous Maze was added soon afterwards, in a corner of a section of garden called The Wilderness.

Further alterations took place in the reigns of George II and George III, as the new style of natural garden gradually replaced the earlier formality, but fortunately much of London and Wise's work was left untouched, even by "Capability" Brown, who was responsible for planting the impressive Great Vine, still one of Hampton Court's main attractions.

It was Queen Victoria who threw open the splendid garden to the public. In more recent times herbaceous borders have been added, with marvellous seasonal flower displays, and a rose garden has been established on the site of the Tudor tiltyard. A new Knot Garden, although planted with many species not known at the time, is a reconstruction of this type of garden, so popular in the 16th century.

Garden open all year, daily.

Far left: this statue stands on the broad lawn flanking the East Front of the palace.
Left: the boundary walls of the New Pond Garden date from the 17th century and the garden itself has been restored as closely as possible in period style.
Left above: an attractively bordered sundial, an intimate feature in grandiose surroundings.
Above: the Pond Garden with the Banqueting House. The garden was laid out around 1700 and was redesigned in the present century.

Isabella Plantation. Richmond Park.

camellia collection, dates from the 19th century, as does the flower parterre. Among some impressive trees are a maidenhair and a narrow-leaved ash.

Garden open all year, daily.

· 3 ·

HAMPTON COURT PALACE
East Molesey

Special feature – see page 44.

· 4 ·

ISABELLA PLANTATION
Richmond Park

Originally planted in 1840, this lovely woodland garden in Richmond Park, with two streams and two small lakes, is at its best in May and early June when the rhododendrons and evergreen camellias are in bloom, creating a continuous blaze of colour along the streamside walks and in the glades. The magnolias, hostas, astilbes and ferns are just a few of the attractive moisture-loving plants.

Open all year, daily.

· 5 ·

ROYAL BOTANIC GARDENS
KEW
Richmond

Special feature – see page 48.

· 6 ·

QUEEN MARY'S ROSE GARDEN
Regent's Park

This exceptionally beautiful and well-planted rose garden was laid out in 1932. The original circle of beds remains, surrounded by pergolas, and new beds run down one side of the

Above: *Queen Mary's Garden, Regent's Park.*
Left: *Syon Park.*

small lake to the park gates, and along an avenue beside the open-air theatre.

Open all year, daily.

· 7 ·
SYON PARK
Brentford, Middlesex

Only the long lake and perhaps some clumps of trees survive of the landscape created by "Capability" Brown for his friend the Duke of Northumberland in the 1770s. The conservatory with its glazed dome and curved wings was designed in the 1820s by Charles Fowler and originally heated by underfloor air ducts. But the exhibition garden to be seen today dates from the 1960s, with the creation of a magnificent 2.5-hectare (6-acre) rose garden and the planting of herbaceous perennials beside the lake. Since then buildings have been put up for special gardening exhibits and there is an extensive garden centre.

Garden open all year, daily.

·5·
Royal Botanic Gardens, Kew

Richmond

The world-famous pleasure gardens at Kew, situated south of the River Thames, cover an area of about 120 hectares (300 acres). Originally there were two separate gardens on this site, one belonging to Kew House, the other to Richmond Lodge, neither of which still stands. Kew House was at one time the home of Frederick, Prince of Wales, son of George II, and his wife Augusta. Richmond Lodge, near by, was the occasional country seat of Frederick's son, George III, and Queen Caroline.

After the death of her husband, Augusta proceeded to lay out her garden with the assistance of one of the leading architects and garden

*The Royal Botanic Gardens at Kew were opened to the public in 1840. The gardens cover some 300 acres and offer visitors a varied display of plants both in the open and under glass. The Palm House **(top left and right)** contains a wealth of tropical and subtropical species. An interesting feature of the Queen's Garden, reconstructed in 17th century style, is the mount with its wrought iron pavilion **(above).***

designers of the day, Sir William Chambers. As a young man Chambers had travelled in the East and his early enthusiasm for oriental culture was reflected in the Chinese-style pagoda 50m (163ft) high, which he built in only six months. The 80 dragons which originally adorned the roofs and eaves have not survived, and all that this quaint building contains inside is a flight of stairs. Chambers added a number of other decorative buildings at Kew, notably some small classical temples, pavilions, and an orangery.

The widowed Augusta indulged her lifelong interest in gardening and gave it practical expression both in approving the overall design and planning the contents, for it was she who initiated Kew's wonderful botanical collection.

At Richmond Lodge George III subsequently called in "Capability" Brown to redesign both gardens, which he had amalgamated. Brown pulled down some of Chambers's architectural features and accentuated the landscape effect, laying out the Long Lake and creating the lovely dell nowadays planted with rhododendrons.

In 1840 the Royal Botanic Gardens were officially established and taken over by the nation. In the ensuing years they were redesigned and expanded, with a new main walk, an arboretum, and splendid avenues of oak and ilex (the latter giving a view across the river to Syon House). Between 1844-8 the great Palm House was built, to designs by Decimus Burton. The building was the biggest in the country – 110m (362ft) long and 20m (66ft high) – with 4,180m^2 (45,000 sq. ft) of glass, and was remarkable for its advanced design.

The immense glasshouse accommodates a wide range of tender and tropical plants, and more recently many other greenhouses have been built, for cacti, succulents, ferns, alpines, Australian species, orchids, etc.

As in all great gardens, there is abundant colour at all seasons, although the soil is not good enough to support really tall specimen trees. Daffodils and cherry blossom start off the year in style, and from then on the tulips, rhododendrons, azaleas, roses and bedding plants provide continuous beauty until the autumn.

One part of Kew that is not universally known but well worth seeing is the Queen's Garden behind Kew Palace, a delightful reconstruction of a 17th-century garden, complete with steps, statuary, gazebo, flowered parterre, sunken herb garden, and wrought iron pavilion on top of a mount.

Kew is chiefly important for its botanical research and education facilities, but for millions it is simply a place of beauty, pleasure and relaxation.

Gardens open all year, daily.

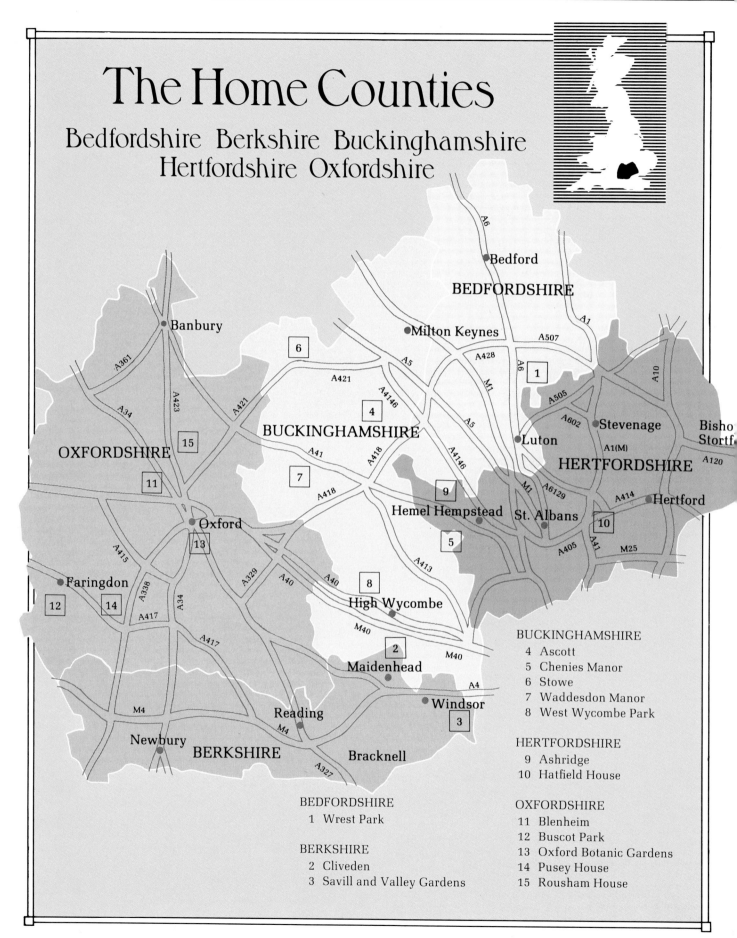

The Home Counties

Bedfordshire Berkshire Buckinghamshire Hertfordshire Oxfordshire

BEDFORDSHIRE
- 1 Wrest Park

BERKSHIRE
- 2 Cliveden
- 3 Savill and Valley Gardens

BUCKINGHAMSHIRE
- 4 Ascott
- 5 Chenies Manor
- 6 Stowe
- 7 Waddesdon Manor
- 8 West Wycombe Park

HERTFORDSHIRE
- 9 Ashridge
- 10 Hatfield House

OXFORDSHIRE
- 11 Blenheim
- 12 Buscot Park
- 13 Oxford Botanic Gardens
- 14 Pusey House
- 15 Rousham House

BEDFORDSHIRE

· 1 ·
WREST PARK
nr Silsoe

The gardens, taken as a whole, make a grand impression, but in fact reflect a succession of periods and styles. They were first laid out early in the 18th century as sections of woodland with a complex network of rides terminated by eye-catching features such as a Roman altar, urns, statuary, etc. The woods flank the long canal with tall trees on either side, culminating in a domed pavilion designed by Thomas Archer, with trompe l'oeil work inside. "Capability" Brown made some alterations but did not change the original scheme; he surrounded the garden with an artificial river issuing from a rustic bath house. One of the bridges across the stream is his, the other, a hump-backed Chinese-style bridge, was added in 1874 as part of an oriental garden. In front of the house terrace are 19th-century matching parterres with statuary and clipped Portuguese laurels. There is a walled garden and a rose garden.

Garden open April to Sept., weekends.

Savill Garden. Windsor.

BERKSHIRE

· 2 ·
CLIVEDEN
nr Maidenhead

Special feature – see page 52.

· 3 ·
SAVILL AND VALLEY GARDENS
Windsor

The Savill Garden in Windsor Great Park, one of the finest natural gardens created in the present century, was

·2·
Cliveden

nr Maidenhead, Berkshire

The diarist John Evelyn, visiting the house and gardens of Cliveden in 1679, described the estate enthusiastically as "... a romantic object, and ... altogether answers the most poetical description that can be made ... on the platform is a circular view to the utmost verge of the horizon, which with the serpenting of the Thames is admirably surpassing". That house, built for the Second Duke of Buckingham in 1666, is no longer there. Both it and the second house on the site, were destroyed by fire, to be replaced by the present Victorian building in 1850. But Evelyn's "platform", William Winde's 122m (400ft)-long brick terrace, is still there; and it still affords a splendid view over the lawn and through the trees to the river.

Cliveden was subsequently acquired by various other noble owners and was leased in the mid-18th century to Frederick, Prince of Wales. Plantings during that century partially enclosed the former open vista with woodland slopes.

In 1893 Cliveden was purchased by William Astor, later First Viscount Astor, who made his own alterations to the garden before taking up residence at Hever Castle, when he handed over the property to his son.

The most remarkable and impressive feature

Above: the Yew Walk leading down to the Thames.
Right: the Parterre with its broad stretch of lawns and box-bordered flower beds gives sweeping views of the countryside.
Above, far right: the Long Garden, with its formal box hedges, topiary and statues.
Centre: the Fountain of Love.
Below, far right: the Water Garden and island pagoda, made for the Paris Exhibition of 1867.

of the present garden, which since 1942 has been administered and developed by the National Trust, is the enormous parterre beneath the house and terrace – a vast expanse of lawn, curving in an arc at the far end, punctuated with a pleasingly simple pattern of beds lined with clipped box.

The First Lord Astor indulged his taste for classicism by filling the garden with statuary, sarcophagi, well-heads, urns and vases. His most ambitious addition was the magnificent 17th-century balustrade below the terrace, brought from the Villa Borghese in Rome.

There is much else to see at Cliveden, most of it relatively informal, but with a number of unusual and surprising features. A considerable part consists of woodland underplanted with various flowering shrubs and including a beautiful valley of rhododendrons, particular Astor favourites. Near this is a water garden, surrounded by more rhododendrons, magnolias and cherries. A Japanese garden, laid out around a small lake, features a brightly coloured island pagoda made for the Paris Exhibition of 1867, topped by a little dragon. The woodland path curves back to the main grass avenue, at the head of which is a huge marble fountain in the shape of a cockleshell with female figures. Leading from this to the opposite side of the house is a path to the Blenheim Pavilion, built in memory of the First Duke of Marlborough. Other interesting features on this west side are an open-air theatre, an Italian garden which has been converted into a World War I cemetery, and a temple made into a chapel where the First Viscount Astor is buried. From here there is a yew-lined walk down to the river.

Garden open March to Dec., daily. NT

devised and planned by Sir Eric Savill, the deputy ranger of the park. The original intention in 1932, when work started, was to make a simple bog and water garden in a glade through which flowed a stream; but after the war it was enlarged to over 8 hectares (20 acres) and provided with many new and interesting features, including a high brick wall to simulate a house. It now contains a wonderful variety of shrubs, flowers and trees, providing colour at all seasons. Sir Eric's original woodland glade has been informally planted, though cultivated with the same care as the formal parts, which comprise a terrace with raised beds for alpines, a fine rose garden with a special section for old-fashioned species, and long herbaceous borders. Naturalized crocuses and daffodils, and waterside primulas mingling with primroses and bluebells, make the gardens a joy in spring, and these are followed by magnificent rhododendrons, azaleas, magnolias and camellias. The herbaceous borders and roses continue through the summer, and in autumn the woodland foliage tints are predictably superb.

The Valley Gardens, extending for nearly 80 hectares (200 acres), were a post-war addition, providing the opportunity for varied landscape development on the north side of Virginia Water. They consist of a series of small natural gardens set in valleys. Here, too, the rhododendrons are especially fine, and there are marvellous deciduous and evergreen azaleas, as well as other shrubs, in the Azalea Valley and the Punchbowl, the latter quite spectacular in summer with its banks of flowering shrubs, maples and conifers.

Gardens open all year, daily.

BUCKINGHAMSHIRE

· 4 ·
ASCOTT
Wing

The Chelsea nursery firm of James

Veitch and Son made this garden at the end of the 19th century for Leopold de Rothschild, and since 1950 it has been maintained by the National Trust. Although there are various formal features, the overwhelming impression is of endless variety and colour, with magnificent trees and shrubs, yew hedges, borders and bedding. The house stands above the terraces, one of which, the Madeira Walk, shelters tender plants. Nearby is a circular garden with a pool and fountain of Venus in a shell chariot, with attendants and dolphins. Another garden contains a topiary sundial, with Roman numerals and inscription, in clipped yew and box. There is a Dutch garden, two rock gardens (one of tufa stone), and a lily pond with a summerhouse. With its combination of formal and informal features, and its splendid

Above: *Valley Gardens, Windsor.*
Right: *Stowe, Palladian Bridge.*

---

views over the Vale of Aylesbury, this is a lovely place at all seasons.

Garden open April to Sept., Tues. to Sun. NT

· 5 ·
CHENIES MANOR
Chenies

The gardens of this medieval manor specialize in roses and old-world flowers. Small enclosures include a physic garden, a white garden, a sunken garden and a 16th-century maze.

Open April to Oct., Wed., Thurs.

· 6 ·
STOWE
nr Buckingham

The extensive landscape garden at Stowe, developed over a period of some 70 years, from about 1710 to 1780, is one of the finest anywhere, a testament to the genius of William Kent. It was originally laid out for the First Lord Cobham by Sir John Vanbrugh (who enlarged the late 17th-century house) and Charles Bridgeman in the formal manner, with a canal, radiating avenues, parterres, pools and classical buildings, notably Vanbrugh's Rotunda, an open domed temple which formed the focal point of the design. In the 1730s William Kent transformed the garden, as he had done at Rousham, by doing away with much of Bridgeman's work, opening up the landscape to follow the land's natural contours, and creating a series of beautiful vistas in which classical buildings of his own design played an essential role.

The wooded valley known as the Elysian Fields incorporates much of Kent's most inspired work. On one side of an irregularly shaped pond he set up his Temple of Ancient Virtue, an Ionic temple with a circular colonnade, considered his finest example of garden architecture. On the other side he placed a Temple of the British Worthies, with alcoves for busts of famous people including Queen Elizabeth, Shakespeare, Bacon and Milton. Among other buildings added later were James Gibb's Temple of Friendship, the Gothic Temple and the Temple of Concord and Victory, the last on the fringe of the open Grecian Valley which was "Capability" Brown's subsequent contribution to the garden.

The Palladian Bridge which spans the narrow head of the Octagon Lake is one of three such bridges in England, the others being at Wilton and Bath. South of the lake is Kent's delightful Pebble Alcove, with colourful animal mosaics, recently restored; and among other features too numerous to mention are the Shell Bridge across the artificial river in the Elysian Fields, the Cobham Monument, and the great Corinthian Arch on the hillside beyond the lakes.

Garden open briefly end-March, then mid-July to beginning Sept., Fri. to Sun.

·7·
WADDESDON MANOR
nr Aylesbury

The ornate mansion, built in French Renaissance style from 1877-83 for Baron Ferdinand de Rothschild, a noted collector of fine art, is situated on a flattened plateau on top of a steep, conical hill, commanding broad views of the surrounding parkland with its fine cedars, limes and beeches, and a herd of Sika deer. The baron also engaged a French designer, M. Lainé, to lay out the formal garden around the house, decorating it with fountains, pools and statuary. The south terrace parterre is particularly imposing with its central basin and Italian-style lead fountain, and is flanked by hedges and balustrades. The spring and summer displays, with thousands of tulips, wallflowers and geraniums, are quite spectacular, and the shows of bedding plants and shrubs in other parts of the garden are equally colourful.

One of the parterres accommodates the huge aviary, in 17th-century style, which is the garden's most original attraction. This consists of a series of handsome pavilions in intricate metal latticework, the central one containing a marble fountain and statuary, and the grey paint is offset by the planting of masses of white "Iceberg" roses. Built in 1889, it was restored by the National Trust in 1966. It houses a wide range of birds, and macaws fly freely all around. The theme is echoed by bird and animal sculptures on the lawns.

Garden open mid-March to mid-Oct., daily except Mon., Tues. NT

·8·
WEST WYCOMBE PARK
West Wycombe

The Palladian house, begun around 1710, once belonged to Sir Francis Dashwood, founder of the Hell Fire Club, which met here. He was the inspiration for the gardens, which were the work of various designers and architects, and which are a fine example of the transition from the 17th-century semi-formality to 18th-century landscaping, with a stream dammed to form a lake, cascades, islands, classical buildings and specimen trees. Thomas

Cook, a pupil of "Capability" Brown added many new architectural features to the earlier work of Morise Jolivet, including Nicholas Revett's beautiful Temple of Music, on an island in the lake above a cascade, and an elegant Temple of the Winds. Humphry Repton worked here for a short time but made few changes, and since no great alterations were made in Victorian times, the landscaped effect remains virtually unspoiled. Once of the contributions of the National Trust, which has administered the property since 1943, is the reconstructed Temple of Venus.

Garden open June, Mon. to Fri., July and Aug., daily except Sat.; also Easter, Bank Holidays. NT

Waddesdon Manor, Aviary.

HERTFORDSHIRE

·9·
ASHRIDGE
nr Berkhamsted

The enormous grey stone house, dating from 1815, belonged to the Seventh Earl of Bridgewater who commissioned Humphry Repton to design the garden. Departing from his usual landscape manner, Repton laid out a series of small formal gardens to the south of the house, one of which, the Monk's Garden, remains; this is a parterre of clipped box with a cast-iron monument. The Rosarie, a circular, hedged rose garden also dates from his time. Newer features include the Lazell-Block Garden, which contains a limestone rock garden, and a sunken rose

garden on the site of a former skating pond. Elsewhere is a fernery, a flint tunnel opening into a grotto, a smaller rose garden with two clipped beech tree-houses, and the Bible Garden – a circle of incense cedars around a stone bible. The extensive woodlands and the arboretum contain a wide collection of trees, rhododendrons and other shrubs.

Garden open April to Oct., Sat., Sun.

·10·
HATFIELD HOUSE
Hatfield

The palace where Queen Elizabeth I lived as a girl, of which only one wing remains, lies apart from the mansion built in 1609-11 by Robert Cecil, First Earl of Salisbury. John Tradescant designed the original terrace gardens and there were additions in the 19th century, including the famous maze. The park and avenues of trees to the north and south of the house create a sense of grandeur, but the formal gardens near the house are more intimate and, although planted mainly in the present century, are redolent of Tudor times. On either side of a lime walk are two parterres, one with flower beds, a water basin and fountain, enclosed by yew hedges, the other used as a rose garden. To the south is a woodland garden planted with rhododendrons, azaleas, cherries, etc. The square garden to the east of the house, leading to the maze, is open once a week.

Garden open late March to mid-Oct., West Gardens and park daily, East Gardens Mon.

Hatfield House, Knot Garden.

OXFORDSHIRE

·11·
BLENHEIM PALACE
Woodstock

Special feature – see page 58.

·12·
BUSCOT PARK
nr Faringdon

The grounds stretch east and west of the house, built in 1780 but enlarged a century later by Lord Faringdon, who engaged Harold Peto as architect for a new formal garden. Peto's imaginative water garden links the house with a large lake to the east by means of balustraded steps down a long, straight

·11·
Blenheim Palace

Woodstock, Oxfordshire

Queen Anne and her Parliament gave Blenheim Palace as a gift to John Churchill, First Duke of Marlborough, to celebrate his victory over the French forces of Louis XIV in 1704. Sir John Vanbrugh, the famous dramatist and architect, designed the palace, and many of the greatest artists and craftsmen of the day helped to decorate it. He never completed it, for the Marlboroughs fell from favour and had to find the money to finish both the house and gardens themselves. Initially, however, Henry Wise, the queen's personal gardener, designed a garden in the baroque style that was fashionable in France and Germany, complete with parterres, ponds and fountains. The magnificent south-front parterre was laid out in curving scroll patterns, with interspersed clipped hedges.

Vanbrugh himself helped to plan the grounds, building triumphal arches and constructing an immense stone bridge, high and spacious enough to contain a number of rooms, to span the River Glyme. Unfortunately the river was little more than a meandering stream, and although a canal was dug, this hardly helped to increase the volume and flow, so that the bridge was literally left high and dry.

Some 50 years later, in 1764, the renowned "Capability" Brown was summoned to Blenheim to landscape the park in the style that had meanwhile become fashionable. Brown began his work of transformation by damming the little river and converting Vanbrugh's canal into a large lake. In the process the lower part of the great bridge was flooded, so that it was only half the height, but so restored to more suitable

proportions. He also did away with Wise's elaborate parterres, extending the vast expanse of lawn up to the palace walls, and planting belts and clumps of trees at intervals for visual effect. With its tree-lined avenues, smooth lawn and shimmering lake, the park remains one of his undisputed landscape masterpieces.

No more major changes were made to the garden until the present century, when the Ninth Duke of Marlborough called in the French garden designer Achille Duchêne to restore something of the formal early 18th-century elegance. The result can be seen today in the terraces on two sides of the palace. To the east is a formal garden with geometrical patterns of flower beds, clipped bushes, neat paths, statuary and fountains. On the west front, facing part of the lake, is an even more original conception, the water parterre, with a series of pools and decorative fountains. To the south, on the site of Wise's parterre, is a sweep of lawn.

The combination of baroque formality, as reconstructed by Duchêne, and the natural beauty of "Capability" Brown's inspired landscaping, makes an overwhelming impression. But there is yet another pleasure in store. Out of sight of the palace, hidden from the lake, is a delightful woodland walk with trees and flowering shrubs – rhododendrons, azaleas, hydrangeas, hostas and many other plants – and a rose garden. It is all very intimate and informal, a charming contrast to the impressive and large-scale grandeur of the park.

Gardens open mid-March to Oct., daily.

Below, far left: *bird topiary in the Italian Garden.*
Centre, far left: *the lower terrace seen from the west front of the palace, with the Bernini Fountain, a model for the fountain in the Piazza Navona, Rome.*
Above: *the Great Parterre on the upper terrace.*
Centre left: *Vanbrugh's Grand Bridge, partially flooded but more pleasingly proportioned thanks to the creation of "Capability" Brown's lake.*
Centre right: *the Mermaid Fountain in the Italian Garden.*
Left: *the Italian Garden and the Orangery, overlooked by the east front of the palace.*

woodland avenue. There are architectural features such as sculptures and jars, down its entire length, flanked by a tunnel of trees, and a stream which follows its course and sometimes moves so slowly as to appear quite still, and elsewhere tumbles swiftly over cascades, into pools and under bridges, narrowing and widening until it reaches the lake, with its small temple on the far bank. Other parts of the garden, added more recently, include beech, poplar and sycamore avenues, and more statuary and ornamentation, but Peto's walk remains the central attraction. National Trust since 1948.

Garden open April to Sept., Wed. to Fri., also second and fourth Sat. and Sun. each month. NT

·13·
OXFORD BOTANIC GARDENS
Oxford

This charming little garden, tucked peacefully off the High Street, is the oldest of its kind in Britain, founded in 1621. The beds of the main garden are filled with shrubs and herbaceous plants, and climbing plants festoon the walls. South of the walled garden is a water garden, a rock garden, a rose garden, a rose border, a big herbaceous border and further collections of shrubs, as well as large specimen trees. There is a fine greenhouse containing an attractive array of water lilies and a wide range of other plants.

Open all year, daily.

Above: *Pusey House, herbaceous border.*
Right: *Oxford Botanic Gardens.*

·14·
PUSEY HOUSE
Pusey, nr Faringdon

The house dates from 1748 and its original landscape garden included a long, narrow lake with a Chinese-style bridge, a temple, a lawn extending up to the house walls, and a tree-framed vista of the countryside. When Mr and Mrs Michael Hornby acquired Pusey house in 1935 they sensibly retained these delightful features but made an entirely new garden containing an extraordinary variety of roses, shrubs, herbaceous plants and young trees. A south-facing paved terrace was designed by the architect Geoffrey Jellicoe, with plants in beds, containers and on the retaining wall.

The entrance at the side of the house leads to a path with double borders and a grey ironwork gate with the family coat-of-arms. Through this gate is the marvellous double herbaceous border, over 135m (150yds) in length, which is one of the garden's principal glories. The path down to the lake leads first to a fine shrub rose garden, with many old-fashioned varieties, and soon there is a glimpse of the lake with its unique "Chinese" bridge. Painted white, with decorative railings and finials, it is only a few feet above the water which is densely studded with water lilies. There are interesting waterside plantings and at the narrow end of the lake is another bridge, and across it a domed temple in grey stone.

The broad lawn between house and lake is surrounded by fine shrubs, roses and trees. Near the house is a quiet, secluded spot, sheltered by a brick wall, Lady Emily's Garden, named after the wife of a previous owner of Pusey. It is lavishly planted with roses, perennials and climbers.

Garden open April to Oct., daily except Mon., Fri.

·15·
ROUSHAM HOUSE
Steeple Aston

The poet Alexander Pope described this as "the prettiest place for waterfalls, jetts, ponds, inclosed with beautiful scenes of green and hanging wood, that ever I saw". He was referring to the garden laid out around 1720 for Sir Robert Dormer by Charles Bridgeman, with a straight avenue, rectangular ponds and winding paths leading down to the River Cherwell. In 1738 Robert's brother James inherited the property and called in the eminent William Kent to make alterations.

The garden today still represents one of the purest examples of Kent's work despite the fact that some of it is rather overgrown and that the avenue and the stone cascades reflect the taste of an earlier period when French formality was all the rage. Both the surviving cascades in Venus's Vale are by Kent, flanking the pool which he altered from square to octagonal; the lower one has a statue of Venus with swans and cherubs, the upper one is in the form of a grotto, similar to the one he designed at Chiswick House.

Near the house is a kitchen garden and beyond that a rose garden with a round dovecote, but the rest is largely informal, with woodland walks down to the river punctuated by glades, temples and statuary. Classical features at various points of the garden include an arcade known as Praeneste, a huge statue of Apollo, a Temple of Echo, a statue of a lion and horse, a "Dying Gladiator" and a pyramid.

On the far side of the lawn before the north front of the house, the ground drops steeply, and thus much of the garden is out of sight of the house, giving the impression of continuity between the garden and the fields and hills on the far side of the valley.

Garden open all year, daily.

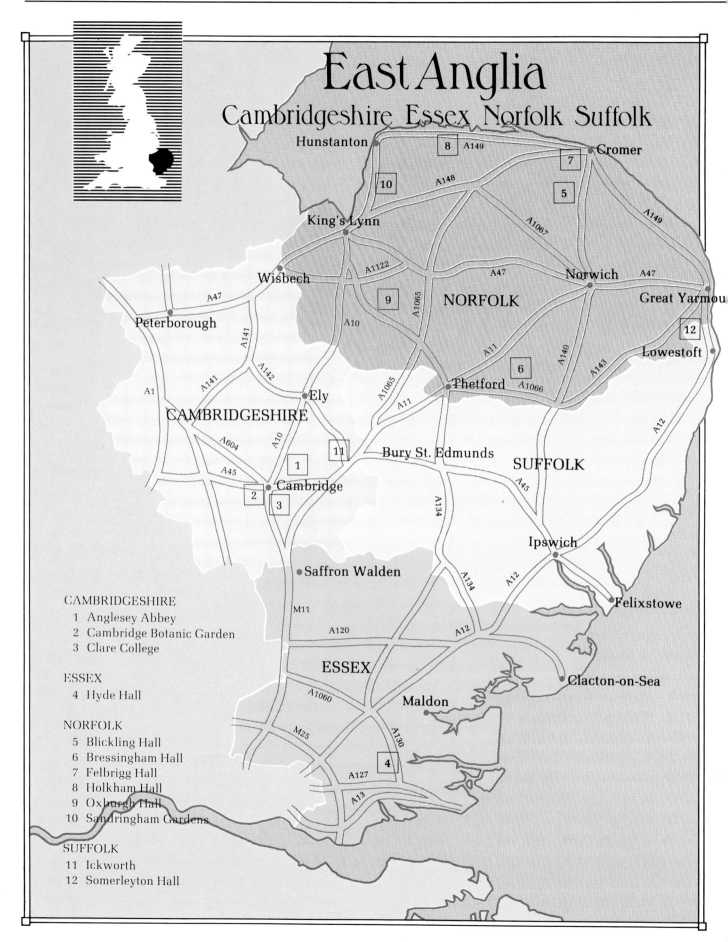

East Anglia
Cambridgeshire Essex Norfolk Suffolk

Hunstanton

8 A149

Cromer

10

A148

7

5

A149

King's Lynn

A1122

A47

A1067

Wisbech

9

A1065

NORFOLK

Norwich

A47

A47

A10

Great Yarmou

Peterborough

A141

12

A141

A142

Ely

A1065

A11

A140

A143

Lowestoft

A1

A604

A10

CAMBRIDGESHIRE

A11

6

Thetford

A1066

A12

A45

11

Bury St. Edmunds

SUFFOLK

1

2

Cambridge

3

A45

A134

Saffron Walden

A134

A12

Ipswich

M11

A120

Felixstowe

ESSEX

A12

Clacton-on-Sea

A1060

Maldon

M25

A130

4

A127

A13

CAMBRIDGESHIRE
1 Anglesey Abbey
2 Cambridge Botanic Garden
3 Clare College

ESSEX
4 Hyde Hall

NORFOLK
5 Blickling Hall
6 Bressingham Hall
7 Felbrigg Hall
8 Holkham Hall
9 Oxburgh Hall
10 Sandringham Gardens

SUFFOLK
11 Ickworth
12 Somerleyton Hall

CAMBRIDGESHIRE

·1·

ANGLESEY ABBEY
Lode

This astonishing garden, now owned by the National Trust, was laid out between 1926 and 1962, mainly to accommodate Lord Fairhaven's remarkable collection of statuary. A series of avenues and walks show these off to advantage, one of the most dramatic being the Coronation Walk, planted in 1937, running half a mile and comprising alternate rows, four deep on either side, of horse chestnuts and planes. The Emperors' Walk, a quarter of a mile in length, is lined with busts of Roman emperors, against an evergreen background. An open Circular Temple of Corinthian pillars, framed by a yew hedge, is guarded by two stone lions and has a marble copy of Bernini's *David* in the centre. Among the more massive statuary groups are those of The Wrestlers and The Warriors, but statues and art objects are everywhere, on lawns and against hedges, placed for maximum effect. A Chinese temple contains a huge polished porphyry bowl. In addition to all this, however, there is an arboretum, a circular herbaceous garden and a flower parterre.

Garden open April to mid-Oct., Wed. to Sun. NT

Anglesey Abbey.

· 2 ·
CAMBRIDGE BOTANIC GARDEN
Cambridge

This is primarily Cambridge University's teaching garden for botany students but it is freely open to the public and contains much of general interest, including excellent roses and tulips, many splendid trees, scented and winter gardens, herbaceous borders and a highly original limestone rock garden. Some beds are grouped so as to display plants of the same family or related families, others to show plants from particular countries and continents. There are numerous greenhouses, equally well stocked with unusual and tender plants.

Open all year, daily except Sun.

· 3 ·
CLARE COLLEGE
Cambridge

This little garden, belonging to the Fellows of the college, is open to the public, and especially delightful in summer when the herbaceous and bedding plants are in full glory; but it is planned for all-year interest, with both straight and curved borders, and well positioned trees to provide charming vistas. There is a splendid metasequoia, an immense swamp cypress and a lovely silver-leaved lime. King's College Chapel is among several college buildings which form an impressive background to the garden.

Open all year, Mon. to Fri.

ESSEX

· 4 ·
HYDE HALL
Rettendon

Bulbs, flowering shrubs, roses and unusual trees provide continuous seasonal interest in this garden on a fairly exposed site near the Essex coast. Eucalyptus, acacias, solanums and

other plants normally associated with warm climes do surprisingly well here, and the greenhouses are well stocked with the more tender species. The rose collection is exceptionally good.

Open April to Sept., Wed., also some Suns.

NORFOLK

· 5 ·
BLICKLING HALL
Aylsham

The handsome Jacobean house, built from about 1615 onwards, is approached by a long drive flanked by simple lawns, affording an uninterrupted view of its decorative facade, with corner towers, gables and mullioned windows. The gardens, now maintained by the National Trust, show the stylistic features of the 17th and 18th centuries, and were redesigned in the present century. North and west of the house is a lake amid parkland, with a pyramid-shaped mausoleum in the distance. Although these are typical of Humphry Repton, whose name is mentioned in their context, records show that this landscape was already there in 1770, before he engaged on his professional career, although the orangery, tucked away out of sight of the house, may have been built by Humphry's son John Adey Repton.

To the east of the house is the beautiful formal garden. This comprises a grassy parterre flanked by terrace walks, studded with flower beds and yew topiary specimens. There is a central fountain and an array of statuary and urns lining the boundary wall on either side of the broad steps that lead up to the raised lawn beyond. Surrounded on both sides by shrubs and trees, this is bisected by a broad path with an 18th-century temple at the end, directly facing the house. At the back of the temple lies an avenue of chestnuts. The dry moat around the house is planted with camellias, buddleia, hydrangeas, honeysuckle and roses.

Garden open April to Oct., daily except Mon., Thurs. NT

· 6 ·
BRESSINGHAM HALL
nr Diss

Alan Bloom was a pioneer of the island bed method of planting, and he dis-

Opposite top: *Cambridge Botanic Gardens.*
Left: *Blickling Hall.*

Above: *Holkham Hall.*

played it nowhere more effectively than in his own garden at Bressingham. By arranging the beds to fit the natural contours of the spacious garden, and filling them with thousands of hardy plants, including rock species, in happy association, he created a scheme which is perfectly integrated and wholly original. The garden has been extended by Adrian Bloom with heathers and dwarf conifers. The result is a lovely garden with a remarkable collection of herbaceous perennials, planted and designed with the utmost imagination.

Garden open May to Sept., Thurs., also Wed. in Aug.

· 7 ·
FELBRIGG HALL
nr Cromer

The 17th-century house is situated about 1.6km (1 mile) from the sea and is sheltered by woods of oak and sweet chestnut. There is a landscaped park, and the walled garden, now filled with flowers, fruits and vegetables, contains a very large dovecote, recently restored. The orangery, built in 1705, has a wonderful display of camellias. There is continuous colour, with an especially lovely array of autumn crocuses. National Trust since 1969.

Open April to Oct., daily except Tues., Fri. NT

· 8 ·
HOLKHAM HALL
Wells-next-the-Sea

The beautiful park was landscaped successively by William Kent, "Capability" Brown and Humphry Repton, although many features have since disappeared. The great lawn, the lake, the belts and clumps of trees and various monuments, notably a towering obelisk, make an impressive sight. The 19th-century terraced garden is generously planted with roses, shrubs and herbaceous plants, and the arboretum contains many rare specimen trees.

Open end-May to Sept., Mon., Thurs., also Wed. in July.

· 9 ·
OXBURGH HALL
Oxborough, King's Lynn

The 15th-century hall and its moat are surrounded by 5 hectares (12 acres) of lawns, flower beds and borders, the last arranged in the form of an intricate French parterre, copied from a design published in 1712. Beyond the parterre is a yew-hedged walk with a long herbaceous border against a wall. The walled kitchen garden contains fruits and climbing plants. Many fine trees have been planted both for ornamental purposes and to give shelter against the fierce winds that blow here. A fine view of the gardens is obtained from the top of a 25m (80ft) tower. National Trust since 1952.

Open May to Sept., Sat. to Wed.; also April and early Oct., Sat., Sun. NT

· 10 ·
SANDRINGHAM GARDENS
Dersingham, nr King's Lynn

Special feature – see page 68.

Below: *Oxburgh Hall.*
Left: *Ickworth.*
Below right: *Somerleyton Hall.*

SUFFOLK

·11·
ICKWORTH
nr Bury St Edmunds

This enormous house, with its high rotunda and two curving wings terminating in pavilions, was built for the Earl of Bristol and only completed after his death in 1830. The garden is simple and geometrical in pattern. On the north side the wings enclose a gravelled court and curving flower border, backed by an oval lawn; on the south is a gravel walk with lawns and shrubberies. One of the terminal pavilions is fronted by a pillared orangery. Many trees were planted in the 19th century, including cypresses and cedars, most of which have failed to survive; but there is still a yew avenue, holm oaks, pines and walnuts. The evergreen shrubs planted at the same time have grown very tall. The garden is now managed by the National Trust and the curved border has been kept bright with roses and shrubs, although the cold climate is not conducive to the growing of tender species. The conjunction of house and garden is unique in conception.

Garden open April to mid-Oct., daily except Mon., Fri. NT

·12·
SOMERLEYTON HALL
nr Lowestoft

Somerleyton was mentioned in the Domesday Book, and the present handsome brick mansion dates from the 16th century, although largely rebuilt in early Victorian times. The 5-hectare (12-acre) garden contains beautiful avenues and specimen trees, rhododendrons, azaleas and other flowering shrubs, glasshouses and statuary. Added attractions for visitors are a maze and a miniature railway.

Open April to Sept., daily except Sat.

·10·
Sandringham Gardens

Dersingham, nr King's Lynn, Norfolk

Sandringham, the most homely and accessible of royal residences, is mentioned in the Domesday Book of 1086 as Sant Dersingham, the first word meaning "sand", the second "water meadow dwelling". Queen Victoria bought it for the 20-year-old Prince of Wales (later Edward VII), who subsequently lived here with his wife Alexandra, having the existing 18th-century house rebuilt by A.J. Humbert in Jacobean style. In 1891 it was badly damaged by fire and additions were made. King George V died at Sandringham, and George VI was born and died there. In the 1960s Queen Elizabeth reduced the size of the house and in 1977, year of her Silver Jubilee, opened house and grounds to the public. Visitors can see the state apartments and walk at leisure around the beautiful gardens except when the Royal Family is in residence.

The gardens have been modified over the years and now comprise park and woodland areas as well as a formal garden. The recommended route leads first to the shrubberies, with rhododendrons, azaleas, camellias, cornus, hydrangeas and many other species. Massed polyanthus provides summer colour and a variety of hostas are planted for ground cover.

The wrought-iron Norwich Gates which cross the drive were made for the Great Exhibition of 1862 by Barnard of Norwich and given to the Prince and Princess of Wales as a wedding present the following year. They were originally placed nearer the house, but were moved by Edward VII after a gale uprooted some of the lime trees flanking the drive that linked the gates and the house.

The formal North Garden was designed for George VI by Geoffrey Jellicoe. It is enclosed with lines of pleached lime trees and divided by clipped box hedges into separate sections, planted in various styles. There is a statue of Father Time and, at the end of the garden, a bronze statue of the Buddhist god Kuvera flanked by stone beasts, known as the "Chinese Joss".

In the rockery above the shore of the upper lake is The Nest, a little summerhouse presented to the widowed Queen Alexandra in

The gardens of Sandringham House, viewed *(top left)* from the Upper Lake, bought by Queen Victoria for Edward Prince of Wales and today seat of the Royal Family, are open to the public almost all the year round. The circular walk through the grounds leads through the shrubberies, the rock garden above the Upper Lake *(left)* and along the path between the Upper and Lower Lake *(above)*.

1913. On the lawn above the rockery, now planted with dwarf conifers, is an old Italian well-head.

To the right of the path running between the upper and lower lakes is an oak tree 850 years old. This is one of the numerous oaks at Sandringham, some of which were planted by members of the Royal Family, one by King George VI and Queen Elizabeth in his coronation year of 1937, another by the present Queen Elizabeth in 1977 to commemorate her Silver Jubilee.

The lake path leads to the Old Norwich Gates, dating from 1724, which originally stood at the main entrance to the grounds but which were moved here when the new gates were set up in 1863. The path then dips to the Dell, a little valley through which water flows to the lower lake, and thence to the exit gate, completing the circular tour.

Gardens open, except for brief period from late July to early Aug., daily except Fri., Sat.

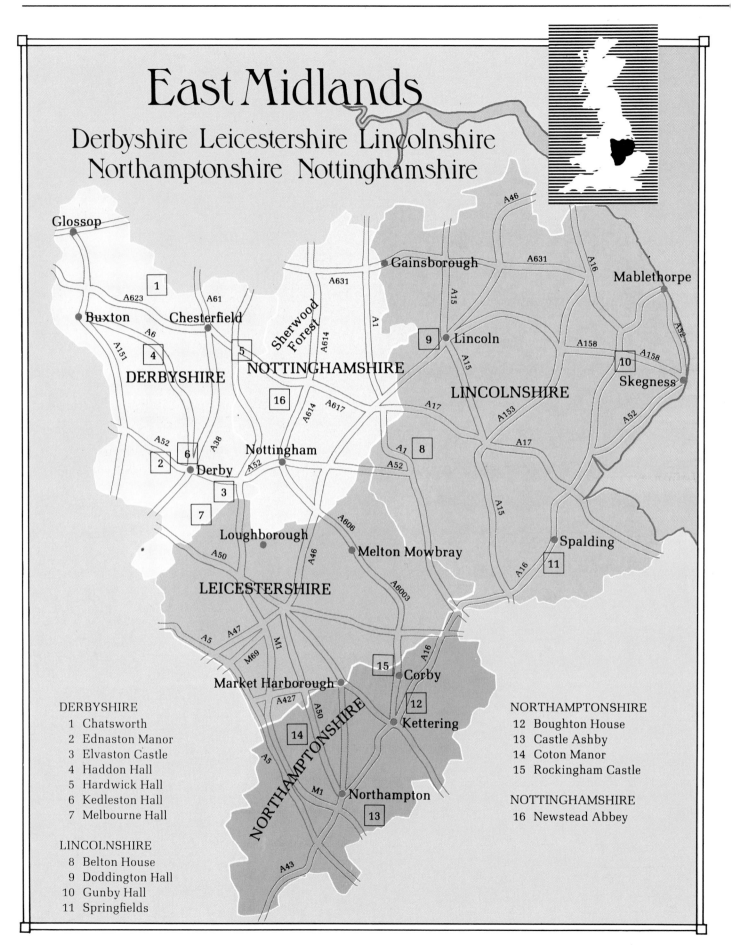

East Midlands

Derbyshire Leicestershire Lincolnshire Northamptonshire Nottinghamshire

Glossop

1

A623

Buxton

A61

Chesterfield

A6

4

A151

A52

DERBYSHIRE

5

Sherwood Forest

A631

A614

NOTTINGHAMSHIRE

16

A614

A617

6

A38

A52

2

Nottingham

Derby

A52

3

7

Loughborough

A50

A606

A46

Melton Mowbray

LEICESTERSHIRE

A6003

A5

A47

M69

M1

Market Harborough

A427

A50

14

A5

NORTHAMPTONSHIRE

M1

Northampton

13

A43

15

Corby

A16

12

Kettering

Gainsborough

A46

A631

A16

Mablethorpe

A15

9

Lincoln

A158

A158

10

Skegness

A52

A15

A153

8

A1

A52

A17

A15

A17

A16

Spalding

11

DERBYSHIRE
1 Chatsworth
2 Ednaston Manor
3 Elvaston Castle
4 Haddon Hall
5 Hardwick Hall
6 Kedleston Hall
7 Melbourne Hall

LINCOLNSHIRE
8 Belton House
9 Doddington Hall
10 Gunby Hall
11 Springfields

NORTHAMPTONSHIRE
12 Boughton House
13 Castle Ashby
14 Coton Manor
15 Rockingham Castle

NOTTINGHAMSHIRE
16 Newstead Abbey

DERBYSHIRE

·1·
CHATSWORTH
Bakewell

Special feature – see page 72.

·2·
EDNASTON MANOR
Brailsford

Sir Edwin Lutyens completed this house in 1919 and designed the east and south terraces. The chestnut ave-nues to the west of the house are also from this period, but most of the planting to be seen today was done later. There are good roses, clematis, rock plants, trees and shrubs, and as the garden has developed a wide range of unusual plants has been collected, giving it exceptional botanic interest.

Open April to Sept., daily except Sat.

·3·
ELVASTON CASTLE
nr Derby

Elvaston is now a Country Park with attractive formal gardens around the remodelled 17th-century house. The large parterre is made of both green and golden box, and there is a yew lychgate. In the adjacent topiary garden is an "elephant" hedge, also of yew. Elsewhere there are woodland paths and an old walled garden with herbaceous plants, shrubs, climbers on the walls, and a good range of herbs. Among the additional attractions is a working estate museum.

Open all year, daily.

·4·
HADDON HALL
Bakewell

The medieval manor, parts of which date back to the 12th century, stands on an escarpment overlooking the lovely valley of the River Wye. The garden is romantically beautiful, with paving, steps and balustrading over 300 years old, and consists of steep hillside terraces, individually designed and planted. The trees on the top terrace had to be felled and are now replaced by lawn, with flower beds and a rose garden. Indeed, Haddon is famous for its roses which are not only formally planted but also scramble freely over house and terrace walls. Above the top terrace is Dorothy Vernon's Walk, named after the heiress who lived here and eloped with her lover in the 16th century. The gate through which she escaped and the pack-bridge where her lover awaited her can still be seen. The second and third terraces are linked by a broad flight of 76 stone steps between a rose-festooned balustrade. All the planting is of the present century and in summer, when the roses are in full flush, the garden is a place of enchantment.

Garden open end March to Sept., Tues. to Sun., except Sun. in July, Aug.

·5·
HARDWICK HALL
nr Chesterfield

This Elizabethan mansion was built for Bess of Hardwick, Countess of Shrewsbury between 1591 and 1597, and the

Haddon Hall.

·1·
Chatsworth

Bakewell, Derbyshire

The spacious and beautiful grounds of Chatsworth, ancestral seat of the Dukes of Devonshire in the Peak District, reflect the changing tastes and styles of gardening over the centuries. The present mansion, on the site of an older Tudor house, was begun in 1687, and the First Duke commissioned the Kensington firm of George London and Henry Wise to lay out a formal garden, with balustraded terraces, parterres, fountains and statuary, on the lines of Le Nôtre's grandiose conception for Louis XIV at Versailles. Of this elaborate garden little remains save a pair of carved sphinxes on pedestals on the west terrace, some balustrading, and part of the spectacular waterworks designed by the Frenchman, M. Grillet; this includes the magnificent Cascade tumbling a quarter of a mile down the hillside into the immense Canal Pool, and the nearby Sea Horse Fountain. They were only several features of a splendid water garden which contained canals and a dozen or so fountains fed through underground pipes.

In the 18th century Lancelot "Capability" Brown, called in by the Fourth Duke, did away with most of these French-style features, widening the River Derwent in front of the house,

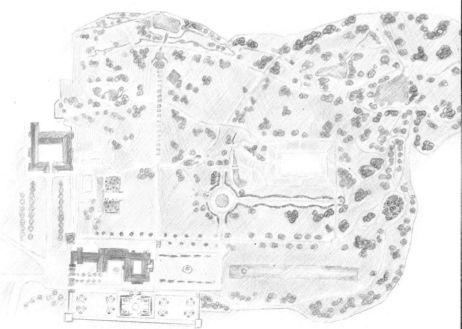

draining ponds and enlarging the park which now swept up to the mansion walls. Judicious planting of trees helped to create the newly fashionable landscape effect that is still admired today by all who come to see the house and its marvellous works of art.

Radical changes were undertaken in the early 19th century when the Sixth Duke, a bachelor with a keen love of gardening, employed Sir Joseph Paxton, subsequently the designer of London's Crystal Palace, to build an enormous conservatory, then the largest in the world, to accommodate a growing collection of exotic plants. The garden was extended with colourful flower beds and large-scale planting of trees and shrubs in the woodland area high above the house. Huge boulders were brought in to create a remarkable rock garden, and a greenhouse for camellias was constructed.

One of the prize specimens in Paxton's conservatory was a giant Amazon water-lily; and this is one of the numerous rare plant species still flourishing in the vast modern greenhouse which replaced Paxton's masterpiece when it was demolished, mainly because fuel shortages made it impossible to heat, after World War I. The present conservatory, designed by G.A.H. Pearce, is equally imaginative, being based on the cantilever principle and modelled on the one in the Edinburgh Botanic Garden (q.v.). The site

of the earlier glasshouse is now occupied by a maze.

Another astonishing 19th-century addition to the landscape was the Emperor Fountain (1843), built to commemorate a projected visit (which never took place) by Tsar Nicholas I of Russia; a single jet spouts water nearly 89m (290ft) into the air. The Willow Tree Fountain, on the opposite side of the house, with multiple jets, is a skilful 17th-century reconstruction.

In addition to admiring the scale and enjoying the delights of Chatsworth's formal gardens, the visitor can wander at leisure along the winding woodland paths behind the house, through the Azalea Dell, ablaze with colour in early summer, past the Pinetum, the modest Grotto and the Grotto Pond, through the Arboretum and up to the Cascade House. The water that spouts from the interior of this temple-like building and from the carved figures on either side is the source of the great Cascade. The paths lead back to the gardens with their roses and herbaceous borders opposite the Orangery.

Natural and formal features blend perfectly at Chatsworth to create a superb and worthy setting for one of the great treasure houses of the nation.

Gardens open 23 Mar. to 26 Oct. daily.

present garden was laid out for Lady Louisa Egerton, daughter of the Seventh Duke of Devonshire around the end of the 19th century. It is thus predominantly Victorian, with later additions between the two wars and, since the mid-1960s, by the National Trust. There is an enclosed garden by the house and an attractive perennial border, but the main garden south of the mansion consists of four roughly rectangular sections divided crosswise by two avenues, one of yew, the other of hornbeam. Two of these areas are planted as orchards, with fruit trees and rose borders, a third consists largely of grass, with magnolias, and the fourth has been developed by the National Trust as a nuttery and herb garden. This contains both culinary and medicinal species, and there are wooden tripods entwined with hops and other climbing plants.

Garden open April to Oct., daily. NT

· 6 ·

KEDLESTON HALL
nr Derby

Sir Nathaniel Curzon commissioned the young Robert Adam to redesign his house and transform the existing gardens. It is one of the finest houses he ever built and the landscaped park provides a worthy setting. The small stream in the park was dammed to form a river-like lake with two islands, crossed by Adam's splendid triple-arched bridge. A small bath-house is also of his design as is the summer-house in the centre of the circular rose garden; and a stone lion on a plinth and a memorial vase to Michael Drayton, the poet, are among the garden ornaments set in place by Adam. The orangery which he designed has been moved from its original position. The pleasure gardens have been recently replanted with shrubs and decorated with fountains. In 1777 James Boswell and Samuel Johnson visited Kedleston and were much impressed by the house and park.

Garden open April to Aug., Sun.

LINCOLNSHIRE

· 7 ·
MELBOURNE HALL
Melbourne

One of the oldest features of the garden at Melbourne Hall is the avenue of pleached yews which through becoming overgrown has now developed into a tunnel of trees. It probably predates the garden which was redesigned by London and Wise from 1704 onwards. This contained a terrace parterre, with alleys, pools and statuary, but prolonged neglect has somewhat obscured the original formality of pattern. Even so, the existing garden has many interesting features. It is broadly divided into two sections, one to the east, the other to the south of the house. The former consists of a succession of lawns bordered by hedges, culminating in a very large lily pond known as the Great Basin. On the far side of the pool

is Robert Bakewell's remarkable Iron Arbour, standing at the axis of the terraced garden and the woodland avenue that runs south. This is a black and gold wrought iron structure with a domed roof and elaborate scrolls and foliage. Bakewell did the work in a smithy on the spot; 20 years later he added the lyre-patterned balustrade on the terrace.

To the south is a complex of radiating alleys, pools, fountains and ornaments. At the main intersection is a huge lead vase by Jan Van Nost, illustrating the Four Seasons on a pedestal. There is another example of Van Nost's work in yew bays on either side of the east parterre – four groups of the twins Castor and Pollux, quarrelling, fighting and at peace with each other. Other figures are of kneeling slaves supporting sundials, and of Perseus and Andromeda. Near the house are plant containers in Victorian basket style.

Garden open April to Sept., Wed., Sat., Sun.

· 8 ·
BELTON HOUSE
nr Grantham

The Wren-style house stands on high ground in 243 hectares (600 acres) of parkland, landscaped in the late 18th-century manner. There is a wilderness garden to the west of the house, with a "Gothic" ruin and cascades; and to the east a splendid avenue of limes leads up the hill to the Belmount Tower, consisting of a huge arch topped by buttresses, obelisks and a balustrade. In the 19th century two new formal gardens were laid out to the north of the house. In Victorian times these were probably quite elaborate but today they are much simpler. The smaller one is a parterre of roses edged with clipped box, and decorated with urns and statues; beyond is a sundial of Father Time and Cupid. The larger formal garden centres on the orangery or camellia house, and has a pool with a large central fountain and grass plots divided by paths. On the east side of the house there is a lily pond and a small temple. Here and to the south there are extensive areas of woodland.

Garden open April to Oct., Wed. to Sun. NT

· 9 ·
DODDINGTON HALL
Lincoln

The lovely late Elizabethan house has undergone few exterior changes but the gardens differ considerably from the pattern in Johannes Kip's engraving of Doddington around 1705, apart from some ancient sweet chestnuts and some original walls. Many fine trees and interesting shrubs have been planted quite recently and the classical domed temple in the woodland garden is actually modern. The spring bulbs and roses are outstanding.

Open May to Sept., Wed., Sun.

Below: *Melbourne Hall.*
Left: *Kedleston Hall.*

·10·
GUNBY HALL
Gunby, nr Spilsby

Tennyson described the garden of this brick house, built in 1700, as a "haunt of ancient peace". The description remains apt, although much is new. The formal garden on the west front, with its sunken lawn, double yew hedges, flowerbeds and sundial date from around 1900, but the kitchen garden is much older, and so are the pigeon house and adjacent garden seat in the walled gardens. Along one side of the walled gardens is a hedged path known as the Ghost Walk, and alongside it a deep pond. There are fine fruits and vegetables, attractive herbaceous borders and excellent roses. Gunby has been maintained by the National Trust since 1944.

Open April to Sept., Thurs. Also Tues., Wed., Thurs. by written appointment. NT

·11·
SPRINGFIELDS
nr Spalding

These show gardens, opened to the public in 1966, are renowned particularly for their spring displays of bulbs and corms, the hyacinths, daffodils and tulips (many under glass) giving sensational colour. Over the years an increasing amount of space has been devoted to roses (well over 10,000 bushes), dahlias, bedding plants, flowering trees and shrubs. There is a forced flower show in February, a maze planted in 1977, and many other entertainments.

Open April to Sept., daily.

NORTHAMPTONSHIRE

·12·
BOUGHTON HOUSE
Kettering

Only a few traces remain of the formal gardens created by the Dukes of Montagu in the 18th century around this medieval monastic building. The park, however, boasts splendid avenues and specimen trees, and once again there are ponds and a fountain. There is a delightful walled garden, rose beds and herbaceous borders; and additional facilities include a play area and woodland nature trail.

Open Aug., daily.

·13·
CASTLE ASHBY
nr Northampton

"Capability" Brown landscaped the grounds of the 16th-century manor, owned by the Earl of Northampton, from 1761 to 1767. This involved changes to the old gardens and the removal of three of the four great avenues; only the 5.6km (3½-mile) south avenue survives. To the north and east of the house Brown created two small lakes and set a temple on the far side of one of them, the Menagerie Pond. He seldom visited the property but is buried in the local church. Victorian additions include the terrace gardens north and east of the house, surrounded by a terracotta balustrade with biblical inscriptions. The orangery, now containing camellias, was designed by Sir Matthew Digby Wyatt and has a raised centre and end pavilions, with a spiral staircase to the upper floor. It faces the Italian Garden, wtih roses and clematis, and another walled garden beyond.

Garden open all year, daily.

Gunby Hall.

· 14 ·
COTON MANOR
Coton, nr Northampton

This charming garden, created in the present century and restored in post-war years, is chiefly known for its marvellous collection of birds, notably ducks, swans, cranes, flamingoes and parrots. The waterfowl are a colourful feature of the pool at the foot of the lawn sloping down from the lower terrace of the house, and beyond the pool is a wild garden with a stream. The terrace along the south front has a wall fountain and a holly arbour at opposite ends, and continues around the east front, where there is a rose garden with a small pool. Elsewhere there are interesting trees and shrubs, but the main pleasure for visitors is to wander through the water garden and enjoy the varied birdlife.

Garden open April to Oct., Thurs., Sun., also Wed. in July and Aug.

· 15 ·
ROCKINGHAM CASTLE
Corby

The castle was built by William the Conqueror as a stronghold and was converted into a house in the 16th century, when gardens were laid out on the north and west sides. Among the features of the west garden was a double line of yews, subsequently clipped into the shape of elephants, and this famous elephant hedge survives to this day. The castle was sacked by the Roundheads in the Civil War and afterwards the keep was demolished and replaced by a circular rose garden, looking much as it does today. There is also a rock garden on the site of the ancient moat. Along one side of the lawn known as the Tilting Ground is an avenue of limes and then the ground slopes down to a wild garden called the Grove, densely planted with trees and shrubs. The simple lawn to the north of the house offers splendid, uninterrupted views of the Welland Valley.

Garden open April to Sept., Sun., Thurs; also Tues. in Aug.

NOTTINGHAMSHIRE

· 16 ·
NEWSTEAD ABBEY
Linby

After the Dissolution of the Monasteries, the Augustinian abbey was acquired by the Byron family, who lived here for almost 300 years. The poet, George Gordon, Sixth Lord Byron was forced for financial reasons to sell it in 1817 and thereafter several owners developed the landscaped park and formal gardens in their individual ways. The oak which the poet planted in 1798 is now a stump in the centre of the lawn leading to the Garden Lake; and from the rose pergola on the far side there is an unrivalled view across the water and back to the house. To the east and south-east there are attractive gardens planted in appropriate style: a Japanese garden, a rock garden, a heather garden, a rose garden approached along a double row of yews, an iris garden, a tropical garden and a Spanish garden. A lawn with statues of satyrs was once known as Devil's Wood, but all the trees have now been felled. By the side of the nearby Eagle Pond is a monument to Byron's Newfoundland dog, Boatswain. North of the abbey is the Monk's Garden, now planted with trees and shrubs.

Garden open all year, daily.

Boughton House.

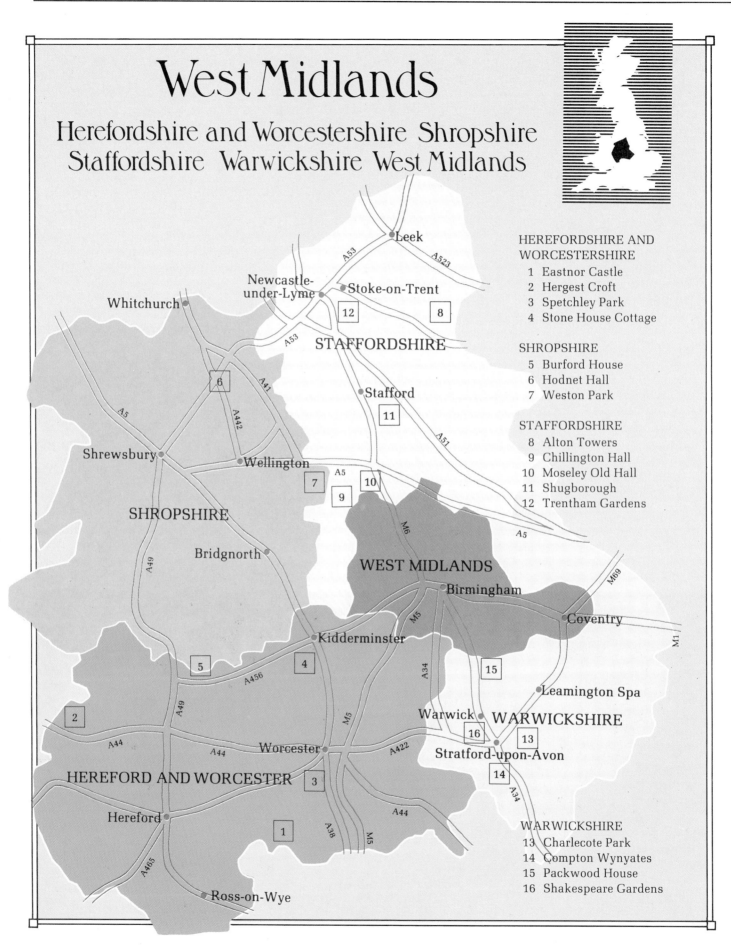

West Midlands

Herefordshire and Worcestershire Shropshire Staffordshire Warwickshire West Midlands

Leek

Newcastle-
under-Lyme

Stoke-on-Trent

Whitchurch

12

8

STAFFORDSHIRE

6

Stafford

11

Shrewsbury

Wellington

7

10

9

SHROPSHIRE

Bridgnorth

WEST MIDLANDS

Birmingham

Coventry

Kidderminster

5

4

15

Leamington Spa

2

Warwick

WARWICKSHIRE

16

13

Worcester

Stratford-upon-Avon

3

14

HEREFORD AND WORCESTER

Hereford

1

Ross-on-Wye

HEREFORDSHIRE AND
WORCESTERSHIRE

1 Eastnor Castle
2 Hergest Croft
3 Spetchley Park
4 Stone House Cottage

SHROPSHIRE

5 Burford House
6 Hodnet Hall
7 Weston Park

STAFFORDSHIRE

8 Alton Towers
9 Chillington Hall
10 Moseley Old Hall
11 Shugborough
12 Trentham Gardens

WARWICKSHIRE

13 Charlecote Park
14 Compton Wynyates
15 Packwood House
16 Shakespeare Gardens

HEREFORDSHIRE AND WORCESTERSHIRE

· 1 ·
EASTNOR CASTLE
Ledbury

The castellated mansion, built in 1814, stands on a hilly, wooded site, and its famous pinetum was created in the main between 1840 and 1880. Early plantings include the firs *Abies bracteata* and *A. grandis*, and among the innumerable specimen trees are redwoods, wellingtonias, incense cedars and the only American beech, *Fagus grandifolia*, recorded in the British Isles.

Open mid-May to Sept., Sun., also Wed., Thurs. in July and Aug.

· 2 ·
HERGEST CROFT
Kington

Near the house a garden with spring bulbs and summer borders is laid out around the lawn. The fine collection of shrubs and trees to be found here is continued in the separate woodland garden known as Park Wood, where the speciality is rhododendrons and azaleas. Among many remarkable trees are rare species of fir, spruce, pine, hickory, beech, ash and maple.

Open May to Sept., daily; Sun. in Oct.

· 3 ·
SPETCHLEY PARK
Spetchley

This Georgian mansion, on the site of a former Elizabethan house burned down by Cromwell's troops in the Civil War, has an attractive garden containing many fine trees, including maples, shrubs and hardy perennials. There is a landscape park, with red and fallow deer, and a lake; and this is linked by lawns and shrub borders to the large walled kitchen garden, sheltered by yew hedges, and a series of more intimate enclosures, formally planted with box and a variety of trees and shrubs. One part of the garden has an old thatched summerhouse and a glass-roofed iron shelter with container plants. There is also a garden centre.

Garden open April to Sept., daily except Sat.

· 4 ·
STONE HOUSE COTTAGE
Stone, nr Kidderminster

This sheltered walled garden covers only 0.4 hectares (1 acre), but contains a good range of herbaceous plants, with many interesting and unusual shrubs and climbers, some of which are offered for sale in the adjoining nursery.

Open March to Nov., Wed. to Sat.

SHROPSHIRE

· 5 ·
BURFORD HOUSE
Tenbury Wells

Water is a significant feature of the highly original garden created after 1954 by John Treasure as the setting for his red brick Georgian house. The River Teme flows past it, feeding streams, pools and the fountain in the centre of

Left: *Eastnor Castle.*
Right: *Spetchley Hall.*

the formal canal pool on the north side. What distinguishes the main garden is the imaginative use of irregularly shaped island beds in broad areas of lawn, and the interesting variety of trees, shrubs and flowers. These are planted most imaginatively to provide striking colour combinations and contrasts and to create a fascinating series of vistas. Annuals and perennials, herbaceous and woody plants are skilfully intermingled to delightful effect. The many species of clematis are particularly notable, some of them being allowed to mix informally with other plants instead of being trained.

Garden open April to Oct., daily.

· 6 ·
HODNET HALL
nr Market Drayton

This garden, with its profusion of spring and summer colour, was planned and laid out after 1922 by Brigadier Heber Percy. By damming a nearby stream he created a series of lakes which are the focal points of a delightful water garden with many moisture-loving plants. Also below the level of the house, with its surrounding formal areas, is the magnificent woodland garden, densely planted with rhododendrons, magnolias, flowering cherries and other trees and shrubs. There are beds of roses, lupins and irises, and great banks of primulas, forget-me-nots, astilbes and heathers. All the planting has been done with great artistry to give a natural effect, and away from the house it merges almost imperceptibly with the countryside.

Garden open April to Sept., daily.

· 7 ·
WESTON PARK
nr Shifnal

The terraces around the elegant Restoration house, ancestral home of the Earls of Bradford, replaced the lawn which was part of "Capability" Brown's park landscape, laid out after 1762. Brown formed two lakes, one visible from the house, the other tucked away in a wood, with a small stone temple alongside. Winding paths

through the woodland are flanked by rhododendrons, azaleas and other flowering shrubs, and shaded by splendid oaks, chestnuts and conifers. At the edge of the wood is the handsome oratory known as the Temple of Diana, from the panels inside that show Diana hunting. The house terraces are enlivened with topiary specimens and ornamental vases, and the gardens and greenhouses contain a good range of interesting plants. The oriental plane, three centuries old, is some 21m (70ft) high, with branches spreading over a circumference of about 122m (400ft). The park offers plenty of recreational facilities, with an aquarium, butterfly farm, miniature railway, nature trails and adventure playground.

Garden open April to Sept.; June to Aug., daily except Mon., Fri., otherwise Sat., Sun.

Hodnet Hall.

STAFFORDSHIRE

· 8 ·
ALTON TOWERS
nr Alton

Special feature – see page 82.

· 9 ·
CHILLINGTON HALL
Codsall Wood, Wolverhampton

Charles II stayed here briefly after his defeat at the Battle of Worcester. The house was rebuilt in Georgian style, and the park was landscaped mainly by "Capability" Brown. There is an oak avenue 1.6km (1 mile) long, an immense lake with bridges and decorative temples, and extensive woods.

Open May to mid-Sept., Thurs., also Sun. in Aug.

· 10 ·
MOSELEY OLD HALL
Fordhouses, Wolverhampton

The garden was created after 1962 by the National Trust, its central feature being a copy of a knot garden made in 1640, its beds edged with box, and the whole surrounded by a box hedge. There is a hornbeam arbour, a nut walk, a small herb garden and an orchard. All the plants in the garden are those that grew in the 17th century, including the White Rose of York and the Red Rose of Lancaster.

Open March to Nov., Sun., also Wed. and Sat. April to Oct. NT

· 11 ·
SHUGBOROUGH
Great Haywood

The late 17th-century house was enlarged, and its park and gardens decorated with monuments, by Admiral Lord Anson, who amassed a fortune after returning in 1744 from his voyage round the world. He brought back from South America seeds of the Blue Pea, *Lathyrus nervosus,* and this flower now blooms in the grounds.

The landscaped park, covering a wide, flat valley beside the River Sow, is dotted, apparently at random, with various Grecian style buildings, including the Temple of the Four Winds, the Lanthorn of Demosthenes, the Triumphal Arch and a Doric Temple. Near the river is the Shepherd's Monument and, on a little hillock, a picturesque Chinese House.

The 19th-century formal garden between the house and the river consists of terraces and topiary work, and a rose garden replanted and redesigned by the National Trust after 1966.

Garden open 15 Mar. to 26 Oct. daily, except Mon. NT

· 12 ·
TRENTHAM GARDENS
Trentham, nr Stoke-on-Trent

There is plenty of entertainment for visitors at Trentham, including a model railway, boating on the lake and an adventure playground; but "Capability" Brown's landscape and the colourful Italian-style terraces are sufficiently good reasons to come here. Brown's 1.6km (1 mile) long lake makes use of water diverted from the River Trent and replaced a smaller formal pool that was prone to flooding. In the 19th century Charles Barry and W.A. Nesfield made the elegant terraces between house and lake, and the beds are filled with seasonal plants. The park contains some magnificent trees, including cedars of Lebanon, firs, pines, wellingtonias, redwoods and swamp cypresses.

Garden open March to Sept., daily.

WARWICKSHIRE

· 13 ·
CHARLECOTE PARK
Stratford-upon-Avon

Charlecote was owned by the Lucy family from the 12th century, until it was acquired in 1946 by the National Trust. In 1558 the young William Shakespeare was arraigned by Sir Thomas Lucy for poaching, and the park still contains sheep and deer. The mansion, which stands in a lovely setting bathed by the River Avon, is Jacobean in style but mainly 19th century; the pink brick gatehouse at the end of the entrance drive is, however, genuine Tudor. Inside the house is a painting of the original mansion and its formal garden. "Capability" Brown partly transformed it, though not in his typical landscape manner, and left the majestic avenue of limes which can be seen today. The garden was further modified in Victorian times, with terraces and balustrades, an orangery, some fine cedars and thousands of annual bedding

plants, but the rustic aviary is of earlier date. The National Trust has recently added and replanted flower borders.

Open April and Oct., Sun., May to Sept., daily except Mon. and Thurs. NT

· 14 ·
COMPTON WYNYATES
Tysoe

This beautiful pink brick Tudor house is romantically situated in a valley, and the view of it from the surrounding wooded hillside is particularly memorable. It was in semi-ruin when Henry VIII gave it to Sir Henry Compton, and both the king and Queen Elizabeth I visited the renovated mansion. It was sacked by Cromwell's troops in the Civil War and almost pulled down to pay a later Compton's debts. The south garden harmonizes perfectly with the house, consisting of fine yew and box topiary specimens, yet it was only planted late in the Victorian era. Since then, ornamental trees have been planted on the valley slopes, and roses, clematis and other shrubs give colour in beds and on walls. There is a small formal garden within the moat area, and a pretty dovecote.

Garden open April to Sept., Wed., Sat., also Sun. June to Aug.

· 15 ·
PACKWOOD HOUSE
Hockley Heath

Special feature – see page 84.

· 16 ·
SHAKESPEARE GARDENS
Stratford-upon-Avon

This little knot garden in Chapel Street is an accurate reconstruction of a 16th-century garden although most of the plants growing in it are later introductions. It lies between a garden on the ruined site of Shakespeare's last home in Stratford and another larger garden where the playwright may have raised fruits and vegetables.

Open all year, daily.

·8·
Alton Towers

nr Alton, Staffordshire

Alton Towers has an international reputation as an amusement park, but not so widely known is the fact that it is one of the most fascinating and imaginative gardens in Britain. It was created early in the 19th century by Charles, Fifteenth Earl of Shrewsbury, and continued by his successors. An immensely wealthy man, without children, Lord Shrewsbury visited his house at Alton only occasionally, and he was already sixty when he decided to lay out a huge landscape garden, with no expense spared. The site was unpromising to say the least, in a steep-sided river valley, a bare and rocky wilderness with poor soil and no attractive natural features. By spending his money lavishly and employing an army of builders and gardeners, Lord Shrewsbury created a wonderland of greenery and floral colour. The River Churnet was dammed to make ponds and lakes, water was brought from a distant spring to feed streams, waterfalls and fountains, terraces and flights of steps were carved out, trees were planted on the hillsides, flower beds and borders were prepared, and the whole garden was filled with decorative buildings and ornaments in a variety of strange forms and styles. The plans were criticized in some

quarters for their "excessively bad taste", and the buildings, designed by several famous architects and dotted about apparently at random, probably made more of an individual impact than an impression of overall harmony. Nor did they blend particularly well with the new gothic-style mansion which Lord Shrewsbury had built by Augustus Pugin, with its turrets, towers and battlements. This is now a ruin, but the gardens, expanded and altered in later years, have become increasingly beautiful; and because the original trees have now grown to considerable heights, they cluster around and partially conceal the Fifteenth Earl's arcitectural "follies" so that each seems a valid, well-proportioned part of the whole. They include a Roman colonnade and bath, a Gothic tower, a Swiss cottage, a stone circle in imitation of Stonehenge, a Grecian temple inscribed, "He made the desert smile", in dedication to the garden's founder, and a Chinese pagoda fountain, situated in the centre of a pool, spouting water 21m (70ft) high.

The gardens of Alton contain a wealth of natural beauty in addition to its special architectural features. The great conservatory is splendidly stocked, there is a marvellous collection of roses in what is called Her Ladyship's Garden, the rhododendrons and magnolias make a magnificent sight in late spring, and the rare trees include cedars, tulip trees and beeches. A large rock garden on a slope across the head of the valley is ablaze with spring and summer colour.

The gardens are situated well away from the popular leisure areas, and can be seen from an aerial railway, although its splendours are better enjoyed, at a more relaxed pace, on foot.

Gardens open end-March to Oct., daily.

Far left: *the Chinese Pagoda fountain, standing in the middle of a pond, was designed by Robert Abraham in 1824. A 70-foot jet of water spurts from the top.*
Left: *the gardens offer a fascinating variety of form and colour.*
Above left: *the Choragic Monument, in memory of Charles, Earl of Shrewsbury, who created the gardens at Alton Towers.*
Above: *the glass-domed conservatories designed by Abraham and later restored.*

·15·
Packwood House

Hockley Heath, Warwickshire

The garden of Packwood House, an Elizabethan building altered in the mid-18th century by John Fetherston, consists essentially of two sections, an attractive walled garden and, beyond this, a remarkable topiary garden. Originally there was one garden on the west side of the house with a curious "Roman Bath", still to be seen, and surrounded by hedges. The other lay to the south, and this was developed in the course of the 18th century to incorporate many of the architectural features to be seen today. This walled enclosure near the house is overlooked by a raised terrace and comprises two long herbaceous borders with a path between. Colour is maintained from spring to autumn with mass planting, and the pink brick walls are also decorated with roses and other climbing plants.

At each corner of the walled garden is an attractive brick gazebo or pavilion, with rounded windows. Although they harmonize pleasingly, they date from different periods. The one in the north-east corner was built around 1680, another, diagonally opposite, in the late 18th century, and the remaining two, matching in style, in the present century. Far from being merely decorative, these little buildings were apparently used – as is attested by the fireplaces in the older pair – as furnace houses in order to heat the adjoining walls, which were formerly covered with fruit, by means of internal flues. There is a further reminder of the past in the series of arched niches built into the wall between the two principal gardens. These alcoves once contained bee boles, or hives, made of straw.

The other garden, reached through an iron gate in the niched wall and down some semicircular brick steps, contains some of the most impressive topiary work to be seen in Britain. The smooth lawn is studded with irregular lines of clipped yew, of varying heights, and the central walk leads directly to a raised mount, which was probably part of the earliest Tudor garden, possibly as an observation point. On top of the mound is a single cone of yew. According to tradition this and the other topiary specimens below and all around represent the Sermon on the Mount and the Multitude.

Unfortunately there seems to be no truth in this story. John Fetherston may well have planted some of them, but during his lifetime they would only have been modest in height, bearing no relation to the enormous specimens that are so admired today. Indeed, it is certain that the majority of these yews were planted only in the latter part of the 19th century. Nevertheless they make an imposing sight, having been well maintained, together with the rest of the garden, by the National Trust.

Garden open April to Sept., Wed. to Sun., Oct. weekends only. NT

*The walled garden of Packwood House **(far left, and above)** contains a decorative pool and statue and gazebos at all four corners. The walls were once heated internally to support the growth of fruit, and the niches formerly contained straw bee hives. Steps from the walled garden lead down to the topiary garden **(top left and right)**. The clipped yew specimens, some of which are supposed to represent the Sermon on the Mount, range in date from the 17th to 19th centuries.*

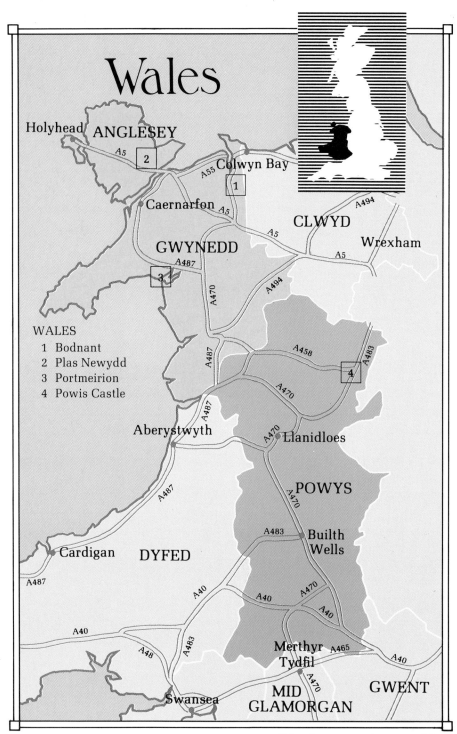

Wales

WALES
1 Bodnant
2 Plas Newydd
3 Portmeirion
4 Powis Castle

down to the strait. The trees include blue cedars and spruces, birches, eucryphias, Japanese maples and magnolias, while in and around the grassy glades are superb azaleas, rhododendrons, viburnums and hydrangeas. It is a place of considerable botanical interest and surpassing beauty.

Garden open April to Sept., daily except Sat., Oct., Fri., Sun. only. NT

· 1 ·

BODNANT
Tal-y-cafn, Gwynedd

Special feature – see page 88.

· 2 ·

PLAS NEWYDD
Llanfairpwll, Anglesey, Gwynedd

Blessed with a mild climate, the garden of the fine mansion owned by the Mar-quess of Anglesey contains a wealth of plants and has spectacular views of the Menai Straits and of Snowdonia. Since 1976 it has been administered by the National Trust. Near the house are sloping lawns, with sycamores and Irish yews, and a little formal terraced garden in which roses hold pride of place in summer. The original land-scaping was by Humphry Repton, who was responsible for much of the plant-ing in the delightful woodland areas beyond the garden proper, sloping

· 3 ·

PORTMEIRION
Penrhyndeudraeth, Gwynedd

The fantastic village of Portmeirion, designed and built by the architect Sir Clough William-Ellis in the 1920s, is now run as a hotel, but it is open to day visitors. Situated in a beautiful cove on the coast of North Wales, this extra-ordinary place reflects the architectural styles of many periods and countries, including an Italian bell-tower, palaces

and colour-washed cottages. There are flowers everywhere through spring and summer – rhododendrons, azaleas, lilacs, hydrangeas, roses, etc. – and the tiny formal park or "village green", with its pool, is surrounded by colonnaded buildings and statuary. Not a garden, perhaps, in the true sense, but nevertheless an astonishing example of fun, fantasy and charm.

Open April to Oct., daily.

· 4 ·
POWIS CASTLE
Welshpool, Powys

The garden of the pink sandstone castle, perched on a ridge overlooking the hilly countryside, is certainly among the greatest in Britain. It is set out in a series of four terraces on a steep slope, each of them of different dimensions and each planted and decorated in an individual manner,

dropping down to the great lawn.

The garden, 137m (450ft) above sea level, faces south-east and enjoys a protected, virtually frost-free position – a perfect site for a marvellous variety of bedding plants, shrubs and trees. The terraces, a harmonious blend of brick and chiselled stone, are decorated with balustrades and statuary and form a vertical pattern in the Italian manner. They make a singularly impressive spectacle from below, dominated by the enormous clipped yews above the top terrace, which were modest little cones when originally planted over 250 years ago. The second terrace, with its arched loggia in brick, is known as the Aviary Terrace because it may once have been an aviary; its balustrade is decorated with lead statues of shepherds and shepherdesses by Jan Van Nost. On the third terrace an orangery, with busts of Roman emperors, is built into the wall.

The big formal garden below the terracing is broken by high clipped hedges and to one side are tall yew but-

Left: *Powis Castle.*
Above: *Portmeirion.*

tresses. There is a good pinetum and the woods in and beyond the garden proper include marvellous oaks and conifers, with two huge redwoods and a Douglas fir reputed to be the tallest tree in Britain.

The National Trust, which has maintained the garden since 1952, has continued the tradition of varied and original planting schemes, and the herbaceous borders and shrubs give a wealth of colour throughout the spring and summer.

Garden open April to June and Sept., Wed. to Sun., July-Aug., daily. NT

·1·
Bodnant

Tal-y-cafn, Gwynedd

The famous gardens of Bodnant, situated above the leafy valley of the River Conwy, with marvellous views to the south-west over Snowdonia, have been developed and maintained for more than a century by the Lords Aberconway, and have belonged since 1949 to the National Trust. In 1905 the second Baron Aberconway decided to transform the steep hillside below the house into a series of terraces in the 19th-century Italian style, complete with lawns, pools, trees, flower borders, balustrades, urns and statuary. Each terrace was individually planned, so that they differed from one another in size, shape, planting and decorative detail. The result was a triumph of imaginative design, and the terracing at Bodnant today forms the most spectacular feature of one of the most magnificent gardens in Britain.

At the top of the slope is the Rose Terrace, guarded by a pair of sphinxes and shaded by two fine arbutus trees. There is a wonderful

Right: the Lily Terrace. The hybrid water-lilies in the pond flower in their hundreds June to September. The huge pond is partially shaded by two magnificent cedars. The buttress wall shelters many rare plants.
Above: beneath the Lower Rose Terrace is the Canal Terrace with a narrow lily pond surrounded by lawn and flower borders. At one end is the 18th century Pin Mill, brought to Bodnant from Gloucestershire.
Far right: the Dell, with its masses of colour in spring and summer, provides a refreshing contrast to the formality of the terraces above.

view of the distant hills from this terrace, which blazes with colour throughout the spring and summer. The steps leading down to the Croquet Terrace are hung with white wisteria in summer, and here again there is a continuity of scent and colour from magnolias, camellias, rhododendrons, lilac, buddleia, eucryphias, hydrangeas and hoherias. The Lily Terrace incorporates two huge blue Atlas cedars planted in 1875, casting shade over the big lily pond which forms the central feature, surrounded by borders of hydrangeas and other shrubs. Narrow steps lead down again to the Lower Rose Terrace with its neatly patterned brick paths and trelliswork pergolas. Finally, there is the Canal Terrace, a complete contrast to the terraces above, consisting of a large canal pool studded with water-lilies, with a yew-framed open-air stage at one end and a handsome little 18th-century building at the other. This is known as the Pin Mill because although originally designed as a gazebo or summer-house, it was later used to manufacture pins. It stood in the Cotswold village of Woodchester and was threatened with demolition just before World War II. The second Lord and Lady Aberconway rescued it, and had it dismantled, transported to Bodnant and reconstructed in its present position.

Behind the mill is a rock garden, with a collection of splendid azaleas, and other formal gardens at different levels contain a rich variety of rare and unusual plants. There is a lovely covered walk of laburnum and a delightful woodland dell in the glen through which a stream gurgles its way towards the Conwy. Conifers and broad-leaved trees cast their shade over the banks of flowering shrubs; here, as in every other part of the garden, there are innumerable rhododendrons, including many hybrids created at Bodnant, in all sizes and colours.

Gardens open mid-March to Oct., daily. NT

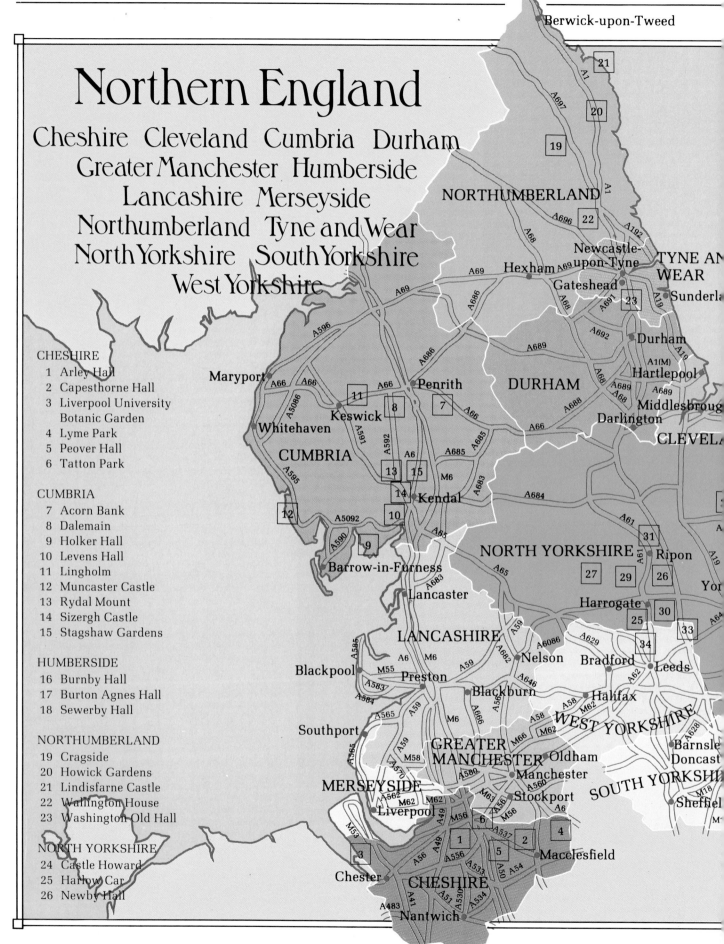

Northern England

Cheshire Cleveland Cumbria Durham Greater Manchester Humberside Lancashire Merseyside Northumberland Tyne and Wear North Yorkshire South Yorkshire West Yorkshire

CHESHIRE
1 Arley Hall
2 Capesthorne Hall
3 Liverpool University
  Botanic Garden
4 Lyme Park
5 Peover Hall
6 Tatton Park

CUMBRIA
7 Acorn Bank
8 Dalemain
9 Holker Hall
10 Levens Hall
11 Lingholm
12 Muncaster Castle
13 Rydal Mount
14 Sizergh Castle
15 Stagshaw Gardens

HUMBERSIDE
16 Burnby Hall
17 Burton Agnes Hall
18 Sewerby Hall

NORTHUMBERLAND
19 Cragside
20 Howick Gardens
21 Lindisfarne Castle
22 Wallington House
23 Washington Old Hall

NORTH YORKSHIRE
24 Castle Howard
25 Harlow Car
26 Newby Hall

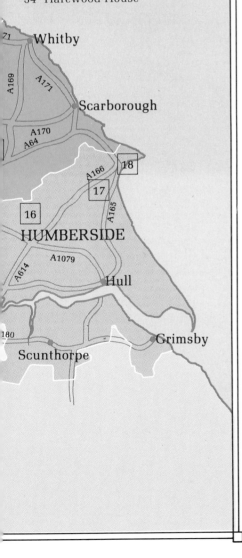

CHESHIRE

·1·
ARLEY HALL
Northwich

The Jacobean-style house is 19th century and the garden is in outline much as it was then, though with modern additions. Particularly impressive are the twin herbaceous borders leading to a decorative stone pavilion, certainly among the first of their kind to be planted. The tithe barn is genuinely medieval. Recent features include a herb garden, a scented garden and a woodland garden. There are excellent old-fashioned and shrub roses, and splendid rhododendrons and azaleas.

Open April to Sept., Tues. to Sun.

·2·
CAPESTHORNE HALL
Macclesfield

The house and its chapel date from 1722, although there were later alterations. Spring and early summer are the best times to enjoy the garden with its daffodil lawn and herbaceous and shrub borders, notably rhododendrons and azaleas, in a lovely woodland and ornamental water setting.

Open April to Sept., Sun. in April; Wed., Sat., Sun. May to Sept.; also Tues., Thurs., July to Sept.

·3·
LIVERPOOL UNIVERSITY
BOTANIC GARDEN
Ness, Wirral

Early in the present century Mr A.K. Bulley founded a nursery, later opened his garden to the public and finally bequeathed it to Liverpool University. Mr Bulley's fine rock garden is still there, and subsequent additions include a splendid double herbaceous border, a long rhododendron border, a woodland garden, a water garden, a rose garden and a magnificent heather garden.

Open all year, daily.

Arley Hall.

· 4 ·
LYME PARK
Disley

The house, parts of which date from the 16th century but with later additions, stands in over 525 hectares (1,300 acres) of moor and parkland with deer and wildfowl, and has lovely gardens maintained since 1947 by the National Trust. The steps and terraces, fountain, glass-roofed orangery and Dutch Garden date from the late 19th century when the First Lord Newton lived in Lyme. The design of this little parterre can be seen from above, since it lies directly under the house walls. Beyond are fine lawns, attractive spring and summer borders and a hedged rose garden. Parts of the extensive grounds are still rather wild but the formal areas have been well restored in recent years. Various entertainments and recreational facilities are also available to visitors.

Open all year, daily. NT

· 5 ·
PEOVER HALL
Over Peover, Knutsford

The gardens date from Elizabethan times and include colourful flower borders, a pleached lime avenue and some impressive topiary work. There are five delightful walled enclosures, a lily pond garden, a herb garden, a rose garden and white and pink gardens. There is also an Elizabethan summer house. The landscape park is typical of the 18th century, and the dell with its rhododendrons, and the large walled kitchen garden are Victorian additions.

Open May to Oct., Mon., Thurs. pm.

· 6 ·
TATTON PARK
Knutsford

Tatton Park, an enormously popular National Trust property, has an exceptionally fine park, partially remodelled by Humphry Repton, with lakes and nature trails, and a splendid landscape garden with interesting buildings. The formal area south of the house comprises a sunken Victorian parterre

Tatton Park.

below a gravel terrace, with a pool and fountain, flower beds and a long balustrade designed by Sir Joseph Paxton. The big L-shaped herbaceous border to the west has a wall on which stand urns, actually chimneys from the flues once used for heating the wall and protecting the fruit trees planted against it. Near by are an orangery and several plant houses, including a fernery designed to accommodate tender ferns from New Zealand in the mid-19th century.

In May and June the rhododendrons and azaleas make a marvellous display, many of them planted around a pool called Golden Brook. Just beyond this is a big Japanese garden, laid out by Japanese workmen in 1910, and thus truly authentic. Its centrepiece is a Shinto temple on an island, connected to the garden by a graceful arched bridge. Stones and water are the principal features of this garden, with stone lanterns, bamboos, pines and an assortment of Japanese plants.

There is a pinetum and many fine trees – beeches, maples and conifers – scattered through the garden, and the walks around the lake are delightful.

Garden open all year, daily. NT

CUMBRIA

· 7 ·
ACORN BANK
Temple Sowerby

Maintained by the National Trust, this is a lovely garden with marvellous spring displays of daffodils and other bulbs, lawns, herbaceous borders, shrubs, roses and fruit trees. The old kitchen garden has been transformed into a garden for herbs and medicinal plants, some familiar, others seldom grown. The splendid oaks along the drive and on the hillside sloping down to the stream account for the garden's name.

Open March to Oct., daily. NT

· 8 ·
DALEMAIN
nr Penrith

The house is medieval, with a Norman pele tower, and in the 12th century there was a simple herb and vegetable garden. The walls surrounding the present formal knot garden, as well as the timber-roofed gazebo, are of Tudor date. The house and the park were landscaped by Stephen Switzer in the mid-18th century, and he laid out the terraced walks and ha-ha walls. The attractive wild garden is part of what was then the orchard, which later reverted to meadow land; this contains delightful riverside walks. There are good herbaceous borders and the whole garden has been restored in recent years, being planted with a wide range of rare and exotic shrubs and flowers.

Open April to mid-Oct., Sun. to Thurs.

· 9 ·
HOLKER HALL
Cark-in-Cartmel, Grange-over-Sands

The large garden of Holker Hall is a charming blend of the formal and the informal and dates mainly from Victorian times. Behind the house is an area of herbaceous borders which is a blaze of colour throughout the spring and summer; and beyond, through a pergola clad with wisteria, honeysuckle, clematis and other climbing plants, is a small, semicircular rose garden, bordered by a balustrade and hedge. The woodland garden, with its winding paths, lawns and glades, contains some splendid trees and shrubs, notably masses of rhododendrons, some of them scented and very rare, azaleas and magnolias. There is a spectacular *Magnolia campbellii* and an immense monkey-puzzle, once blown down but raised back into place by a team of shire horses.

Open April to Oct., daily except Sat.

· 10 ·
LEVENS HALL
nr Kendal

The garden of Levens Hall is famous for its astonishing specimens of topiary, but many visitors fail to take the opportunity of visiting the adjoining park, which is exceptionally beautiful. Architects of both were the owner of the Elizabethan house on the banks of the River Kent, Colonel James Graham, and his French head gardener, Guillaume Beaumont.

The park was probably laid out in the early 18th century, and includes an avenue of oaks 1.6km (1 mile) long culminating in a lovely view of the river gorge. Beeches planted along the edge of the gorge and other tree clumps on the far side show that the avenue was deliberately planned to draw attention to this natural feature. There is also an attractive woodland walk to the river valley.

The garden around the house was laid out earlier, probably between 1690 and 1720, in separate sections, as was fashionable in the Stuart period. There is a rose garden, some well planted herbaceous borders and grassy areas enclosed by clipped beech hedges. The principal attraction of the formal garden, however, is the topiary work. There are specimens in both box and yew, some of them of enormous size and in extraordinary shapes. Many of these were certainly planted at the time the garden was first laid out but others date from the early 19th century. Obviously Colonel Graham could never have envisaged the potentially huge dimensions of the specimens he planted, but shaped and trimmed as they have been over the centuries they give unique distinction to this remarkable garden.

Garden open April to Sept., daily except Fri., Sat.

Levens Hall.

Rydal Mount.

·11·
LINGHOLM
Keswick

Much of this large garden comprises woodland, with magnificent rhododendrons and azaleas, and splendid trees. Near the house a wrought iron gate leads into a rock garden with a pool. The long garden walk affords superb views over Derwent Water towards Borrowdale.

Open April to Oct., daily.

·12·
MUNCASTER CASTLE
Ravenglass

The ancient red sandstone castle stands on a hill at the foot of Eskdale and commands superb mountain views. A long grass walk, with a clipped hedge, overlooks the narrow valley known as the Ghyll. There is a formal garden, with mixed planting, beside the castle, but Muncaster is chiefly renowned for its wonderful collection of rhododendrons and azaleas which, mingled with other flowering shrubs and trees, grow in the valley and surrounding woods.

Open April to Sept., Tues. to Sun.

·13·
RYDAL MOUNT
Ambleside

The house which was William Wordsworth's last home is still owned by his descendants. The poet himself landscaped the 4.8-hectare (4½-acre) garden, which contains some rare trees and shrubs. The informal nature of the garden, blending so well with the countryside around, faithfully reflects the poet's tastes, and the views he enjoyed remain unchanged.

Open March to Oct., daily; Nov. to mid-Jan., daily except Tues.

·14·
SIZERGH CASTLE
Sizergh, nr Kendal

Special feature – see page 96.

·15·
STAGSHAW GARDENS
Ambleside

The rhododendrons and azaleas are outstanding in this woodland garden planted up a hillside. Other trees and shrubs include embothriums, camellias and magnolias. There are fine views over Windermere.

Open April to June, daily. NT

HUMBERSIDE

· 16 ·
BURNBY HALL
Pocklington

This delightful water garden was begun early in the present century by Major P.M. Stewart, a big game hunter and fisherman, who made two large ponds, known as Upper Water and Lower Water, initially for private use but later for the planting of water lilies. This was not completed until about 1950. It is the largest collection of water lilies in the country, comprising many thousands of plants belonging to some 60 species. The small islands in the ponds are planted with water-loving plants, as are the pathways all around. Fish and waterfowl add to the variety of the scene, and in midsummer the lilies, in every shade of yellow, pink, red and crimson, are quite spectacular.

Open April to Sept., daily.

· 17 ·
BURTON AGNES HALL
Burton Agnes, nr Bridlington

The entrance to the Elizabethan house is through the arch of a gatehouse dating from 1610, and the forecourt, part of the original formal gardens, is bordered by ball-shaped yews. Yews in other shapes and sizes are also a feature of the walks and lawns around the house. To the east they form a background to two ponds and a group of statuary, and contemporary bronze statues decorate the lawns. Elsewhere there are herbaceous and shrub borders, a large walled garden with vegetables and fruit, and woodland walks with fine trees and a variety of attractive ground cover.

Open April to Oct., daily.

· 18 ·
SEWERBY HALL
Bridlington

The house stands on the clifftop overlooking Bridlington Bay and the North Sea. The gardens proper lie north of the house and contain a wide range of plants that are both botanically interesting and dazzlingly beautiful. The great lawn is dominated by giant araucarias or monkey puzzle trees, and throughout the garden there are oaks, sweet and horse chestnuts, walnuts, yews and conifers. The formal garden contains flower beds, with a central basin and a statue of Pandora; and a path leads to the walled Old English garden with topiary yew hedges, box-edged paths, herbaceous enclosures and a fishpond with a lead copy of Verrocchio's *Boy with a Fish*. Recreational facilities include golf and putting, and there is a zoo and an aviary.

Open all year, daily.

NORTHUMBERLAND

· 19 ·
CRAGSIDE
Rothbury

There are over 364 hectares (900 acres) of grounds surrounding the enormous house built by the Victorian architect Richard Norman Shaw on the southern edge of Alnwick Moor. The property was acquired by the National Trust in 1977. It is really an immense rock and woodland garden, with wild natural scenery that includes beautiful lakes, streams and gorges, and mile after mile of magnificent rhododendrons and azaleas.

Open April to Oct., daily; Nov. to March, Sat., Sun. NT

· 20 ·
HOWICK GARDENS
Alnwick

The woods near the house provide an ideal setting for a wild garden where rhododendrons, azaleas, magnolias, meconopsis, hydrangeas, primulas, etc.

Wallington House.

·14·
Sizergh Castle

Sizergh, nr Kendal, Cumbria

Sizergh has been the home of the Strickland family for more than 700 years and was built around a massive pele tower dating from 1340 to deter Scottish marauders. The tower is 18m (60ft high) high and has walls 5.75m (19ft) thick at the base. Other additions to the house are from the 15th, 16th and 18th centuries. The grounds, with their lakes and ponds, were laid out mainly in the 18th century. The castle was originally approached by way of an avenue of beeches leading from the gates at the far side of the lawn, but these trees have recently been replaced by hybrid limes. There is a wealth of spring colour around the lawn and formal terraces, and on the slopes above the garden lake, with great drifts of narcissi, hostas and gentians; and the island beds are bright in summer with shrub roses and geraniums. The warm walls that once encouraged fruit trees to ripen now support shrubs of many kinds – clematis, jasmine, ceanothus, viburnum, pyracantha, escallonia, to mention only a few.

The principal attraction of Sizergh, however, is the 0.1 hectare ($\frac{1}{4}$-acre) rock garden at one side of the castle. This was built in 1926, in the naturalistic style then fashionable, by the Ambleside nursery firm of T.R. Hayes & Son, from local Cumbrian limestone, complete with its weather and water markings, and arranged so skilfully as to give the impression that it had always been lying around on this site. The garden is set in a bowl protected by tall trees, so creating a favourable microclimate for an astonishingly wide range of plants; and a little artificial stream tumbles down miniature cascades and through pools into the lake, providing ideal

The castle steps lead down to the terrace and lake, extended from the original moat.

Right: *the attractions of Sizergh include lawns, herbaceous borders, an orchard, a wild garden and the lake. The unique feature, however, is the large rock garden of weathered limestone with its wide range of conifers, including dwarf varieties, aquatic plants and about 120 species of hardy ferns.*

conditions for the growth of moisture-loving astilbes, rodgersias, primulas and other species. Particularly notable are the willow gentians, in white and all shades of blue, which flower in the autumn.

Many of the conifers planted at the time the rock garden was originally created have since grown to considerable height, especially the various Eurasian pines. A proportional growth rate has also affected many of the true dwarf conifers planted for decorative effect in a small dell apart from the main garden. Some of the dwarf spruces are over 2.5m (8ft) tall, and there are unusually bushy forms of the noble fir, cypresses, thujas and junipers, to which pines and cedars have recently been added. They stand out beautifully in autumn in contrast to the adjoining Japanese maples, aglow with scarlet foliage in autumn.

The rock garden is a particular favourite with pteridologists, better known as fern-lovers. Indeed, this is among the biggest and most varied collection of ferns in the British Isles. Only an expert would be able to identify them all and many are known only by their scientific name; they include various forms of royal fern, ostrich plume fern, sword and shield ferns, beech and oak ferns, spleenworts and maidenhair fern, polypodies and many others in a great diversity of structure, tone and texture.

Garden open April to Oct., Mon., Wed., Thurs., Sun. NT

seem to flower as naturally and prolifi-
cally as the spring bulbs. The formal
terraces in front of the house are imaginatively filled with small shrubs,
alpines and other plants.

Open April to Sept., daily.

· 21 ·
LINDISFARNE CASTLE
Holy Island

The tiny 16th-century island fort, high
on a rock over the sea, was restored and
converted into a private house in 1903
by Sir Edwin Lutyens and the property
is now administered by the National
Trust. Gertrude Jekyll designed the
charming little walled garden which is
separate from the castle.

*Open when the gardener is there or on
application to administrator. NT*

· 22 ·
WALLINGTON HOUSE
Cambo

The grounds of Wallington House
cover some 40 hectares (100 acres),
much of it consisting of woodland, and
have been administered since 1942 by
the National Trust. Plans dating from
1737 show an elaborate, large-scale
design with radiating avenues, walks,
canals and ponds. Not much remains of
this grandiose conception apart from
some walks, two ponds in the woods,
and a classical portico in a high brick
wall.

The main garden around the house
comprises lawns, flower beds and an
assortment of trees. It is pleasantly laid
out and well planted but Wallington's
principal attraction is a secret walled
garden (formerly the kitchen garden) in
the wood, designed by the owners of
the estate, Sir George and Lady Trevel-

Newby Hall.

yan, early in the present century, and
later modified and replanted by the
National Trust. The terrace is decorated with lead figures and has flower
borders, a large conservatory containing a good collection of fuchsias, and
greenhouses. Lady Trevelyan's rustic
terrace is bedecked with roses and she
also built a stone niche with a pool.
Ornamental trees are surrounded by
circular beds of flowers, and a rocky
stream flanked by alpine plants and
dwarf shrubs meanders through the
garden, vanishing underground in
places and reappearing a little farther
on. The whole effect is delightfully
informal and quite captivating.

Garden open all year, daily. NT

· 23 ·
WASHINGTON OLD HALL
Washington, Tyne and Wear

This Jacobean stone mansion of 1610, on the site of an older medieval house, was an ancestral home of George Washington. There is a Jacobean garden and a formal garden restored with the aid of American donations. The roses are outstanding.

Open all year, daily.

NORTH YORKSHIRE

· 24 ·
CASTLE HOWARD
nr Malton

Special feature – see page 100.

· 25 ·
HARLOW CAR
Harrogate

This fine garden, created as recently as 1948 by the Northern Horticultural Society, is of great botanic and practical interest, the northern counterpart, in fact, of Wisley. Beautifully landscaped and enormously varied, it covers some 24 hectares (60 acres). Most of this is woodland, including an arboretum, the remainder comprising trial and ornamental areas. There are shrub and rose borders, a rose garden, two rock gardens (one with scree beds), a heather garden, a foliage garden, a stream garden which despite the chemicals in the water contains a profusion of moisture-loving plants, an alpine house, greenhouses and other features. The site was deliberately chosen because of its height above sealevel, its poorish soil and its difficult climate, but the scope of planting, in terms both of quantity and quality, is astonishing. There are literally hundreds of different rhododendron species, for example, and many dozens of species of individual trees and shrubs, including maples, oaks, viburnum, cotoneaster, magnolia, lilacs, hydrangeas and many others.

Open all year, daily.

· 26 ·
NEWBY HALL
. Skelton

Although the house is late 17th century, with alterations in the mid-18th century by Robert Adam, the garden, one of the finest in Yorkshire, is mainly the creation of Major Edward Compton after 1925. Thanks to its varied soil and favourable microclimate, it now boasts a wonderful collection of roses, shrubs and herbaceous plants.

From the south terrace, past a lily pond, a broad grassy path, flanked by two enormous herbaceous borders, forms the main north-south axis of the garden. On either side are small, specialized gardens or enclosures and plantings of rhododendrons and other shrubs in a wild garden. Running from east to west, at the entrance to the herbaceous border area, is the statue walk, a gravelled path lined with grey stone Venetian statues on pedestals, effective against the dark green yews and flowering shrubs. Off this walk is Sylvia's Garden, a sunken parterre surrounded by yew hedges with flagged paths and beds planted informally with pinks, aubrietia, thyme, lavender, lilies, etc. On either side of the long herbaceous borders are a July garden, a rose species garden and an autumn garden. The sunken rose garden, surrounded by a copper beech hedge, contains shrub and old-fashioned varieties as well as other shrubs. There are two separate rock gardens and, towards the river end, an orchard garden and a tropical garden.

Throughout the garden, both in the formal and the semi-woodland areas, there are many shrubs and trees to delight plantsmen, including magnolias, cherries, apple, eucryphias, embothriums and even eucalyptus.

Garden open April to Sept., daily except Mon.

· 27 ·
PARCEVALL HALL
Appletreewick, nr Pateley Bridge

This 17th-century manor house, in a delightful hillside setting, has two gardens, both fairly modern; the wild woodland garden at the back contains spendid rhododendrons, many from China, and the terraced garden at the front has a wide range of trees, shrubs and flowers. There are four terraces, strongly buttressed, leading by flights of steps down to the lawn below. Each terrace is differently designed and planted, two of them with ornamental pools, some with flower beds and all with walls festooned with roses and other climbers. The rhododendrons, azaleas, camellias and fuchsias are particularly fine.

Open April to Oct., daily.

· 28 ·
RIEVAULX TERRACE
Helmsley

This 800m (half-mile) stretch of grassy terrace, made by Thomas Duncombe, whose father and grandfather had previously created similar terraces at nearby Duncombe Park, overlooks the ruins of Rievaulx Abbey in the valley below. It follows a sweeping curve along a wooded ridge so as to provide spectacular views at various vantage points. At one end of the terrace is an Ionic temple, with frescoes and 18th-century furniture inside; at the other is a circular Tuscan temple with a mosaic pavement and coloured plasterwork. Plans to link the Duncombe and Rievaulx terraces never materialized. The National Trust acquired the terrace in 1972 and cleared some of the trees growing on the slopes in order to restore the original views of the abbey.

Open May to Oct., daily. NT

· 29 ·
RIPLEY CASTLE
Ripley, nr Harrogate

From the terraces of the 14th-century castle there are sweeping views of "Capability" Brown's landscaped park with its lakes, cascades and wooded

·24·
Castle Howard

nr Malton, North Yorkshire

Horace Walpole, famous man of letters, described the landscape surroundings of Castle Howard as sublime, its lawn the "noblest in the world fenced by half the horizon". Both the castle and its grounds were designed at the opening of the 18th century by the soldier, dramatist and architect Sir John Vanbrugh and his assistant Nicholas Hawksmoor, both of whom also worked on the palace and park at Blenheim, and here too the nursery firm of London and Wise was involved. The owner himself, Charles Howard, Third Earl of Carlisle, was largely responsible for planning the overall design, and the magnificent landscape garden, laid out on a suitably large scale to match the grandeur of the huge mansion, was the first major example of this new conception, a complete departure from the geometrical formality of the previous century and a signpost towards the later, more naturalistic work of "Capability" Brown and his school.

Set commandingly on an east-west ridge of a hill, with distant views to north and south, the house, with its military-style outposts of gates, bastioned walls and towers, is approached by an avenue of beeches and limes, extending for about 8 km (5 miles). The focal point of the formal area around the house, laid out by London and Wise, is the elaborate parterre. Redesigned by Nestfield in the mid-19th century, it now contains clipped hedges, flower borders, a variety of sculpture, and a large central fountain of Atlas supporting his globe, which was originally designed for the Great Exhibition of 1851. Other areas near the house include a rose

Far left: *the south front of Castle Howard, built for the Third Earl of Carlisle by Vanbrugh and Hawksmoor.*
Below, far left: *Grecian statue on lawn facing south front.*
Below, left: *avenue in the grounds of Castle Howard.*
Left: *the Temple of the Four Winds, a Vanbrugh masterpiece.*
Below: *the south lake and view of the house.*

garden, and there is additional colour from the climbing plants on the south-facing walls of the building.

The Earl of Carlisle's vision extended far beyond the formal gardens immediately surrounding the house, for he planned to transform the whole hillside to the south into a composition of pictorial beauty, notably by adorning the existing natural features with strategically placed classical monuments. To the east of the house the statue terrace continues as a grassed walk, with panoramic views over the parkland below, and terminating in Vanbrugh's inspired Temple of the Four Winds, dating from 1724-6. To the north is a woodland area and to the south there is a view down over the river, lake and stone bridge. Across the lake is a pyramid and beyond Vanbrugh's elaborate building there is another classical masterpiece, the domed temple designed by Hawksmoor, known as the Mausoleum, where the earl was buried.

Castle Howard has recently become familiar to millions of television viewers as the setting for the BBC's excellent adaptation of Evelyn Waugh's *Brideshead Revisited.*

Gardens open end-March to Oct., daily.

islands. Some of the oaks and beeches by the waterside were his original plantings, and the peaceful scenes of grazing cattle, deer and waterfowl create an effect largely unaltered through the centuries.

The walled pleasure garden reached by a path from the north terrace contains interesting architectural features, notably a handsome orangery dating from 1820, with an iron and glass roof, and two balustraded stone summerhouses. There is a fine herbaceous border and ornamentally shaped rose beds. Beyond the orangery a woodland path leads to a four-pillared classical temple, framed by ancient oaks, beeches and laurel, and fine displays of hybrid rhododendrons.

A wrought iron gate in the walled garden leads into a reserve garden with a circular, brick-pillared rose pergola and box-edged parterres planted with lupins, delphiniums and paeonies. A hornbeam hedge divides it from the kitchen garden with its apple and pear trees and cordons of soft fruit.

Garden open end-April to mid-Oct., daily.

· 30 ·
RUDDING PARK
Follifoot, nr Harrogate

The simple, well-proportioned Regency house commands fine views over the Vale of York and across smooth lawns to the belts of woodland that frame Humphry Repton's beautiful landscape. The park, with some old trees and the minimum of ornamentation, is impressively restrained. To the west and south of the house is the new woodland garden, dating from 1945. Formal areas include a parterred herb garden, a walled garden with herbaceous borders and a small brick orangery, and a rose garden. The rest consists of grassy walks among the trees, radiating alleys which at one point converge on a circular clearing with an urn on a pedestal, and extensive planting of shrubs and other plants either in island beds or in groups around the trees. There are individual areas for rhododendrons, azaleas and lilies, and hydrangeas.

Open April to June, daily.

Studley Royal.

· 31 ·
STUDLEY ROYAL AND FOUNTAINS ABBEY
Studley Roger

The picturesque landscape and water garden of Studley Royal was made between 1718 and 1742 by John Aislabie, the Chancellor of the Exchequer who was disgraced but not financially ruined by the "South Sea Bubble" scandal. In a steep, craggy valley of wild beauty to the south of his house (which was burned down in 1964) Aislabie dammed and diverted the waters of the little River Skell to create a series of canals, pools, cascades and fountains, decorating his garden with classical buildings and statues. In front of one circular and two crescent-shaped ponds, known as the Moon Pools, is a long canal pool that tumbles down a stepped cascade into a big lake with a central island, which once boasted a tall obelisk fountain. Behind the Moon Pools, silhouetted against the trees, is a white Doric temple in Palladian style, the Temple of Piety.

There are peaceful walks past the Moon Pools and the lake, one of which leads up steeply through woodland to a grotto tunnel and an octagonal Gothic-style tower, and then past a domed rotunda which, despite appearances, is made of wood. There are lovely glimpses of the river below and then, just before the path descends, a magnificent and surprising view of the romantic ruin of Fountains Abbey, with its spectacular tall tower, by the water's edge. This Cistercian abbey was founded in 1132 by monks from York. John Aislabie had wanted to purchase the ruins but it was his son William who eventually bought the abbey buildings and estate in 1768. He too was an enthusiastic garden designer but by now the taste for for-

designed and with imaginative under-planting. The lower terrace consists of open lawn with a long lily pond.

Open April to Oct., daily in April, there-after Sun. and Tues.

WEST YORKSHIRE

· 33 ·
BRAMHAM PARK
nr Wetherby

This is one of the finest examples in Britain of a French-style garden dating from the late 17th and early 18th centuries, consisting of avenues through woodland, ponds and cas-cades, garden temples and a miscellany of ornaments. Fortunately it remained untouched either by the landscape movement or by subsequent Victorian fashions, although a gale in 1962 des-troyed many of the beeches and other trees that originally framed the radiat-ing avenues. Replanting has gradually helped to restore that original pattern,

and the various temples, obelisks, sta-tues and urns can once more be admired in their intended settings.

Open June to Aug., Sun., Tues., Wed., Thurs.

· 34 ·
HAREWOOD HOUSE
Harewood

"Capability" Brown made the land-scape garden at Harewood House, on terrain somewhat rougher and hillier than was customary for him. He dammed a stream to form a large lake, created pleasant vistas in all directions and planted belts of trees. Near one end of the lake he laid out a "pleasure garden" with a summerhouse; this is now a bog garden, with a Japanese fla-vour to it, and also by the lakeside is a charming box-edged rose garden. Quite separate from all this is Sir Charles Barry's formal garden on the south front, comprising balustraded terraces, three fountain basins (only one of which now contains water), a working fountain, statuary and other ornamentation.

Open April to Oct., daily; Feb., March and Nov., Sun. only.

Harewood House.

mality had given way to the landscape movement, so he merely widened the stream, built low weirs and made some small cascades to give the ruin a suit-ably picturesque setting.

Garden open all year, daily. NT

· 32 ·
SUTTON PARK
Sutton-on-the-Forest

The Georgian house overlooks a land-scaped park with clumps of trees, repu-tedly but not certainly by "Capability" Brown. Behind this, separated by a hedge and balustraded seat, is the attractive terraced garden laid out after 1962 by Major and Mrs Reginald Shef-field, assisted by the eminent garden architect Percy Cane. There are three terraces, the top one paved for sitting out, has twin borders of flowers and shrubs. The second terrace, down steps flanked by bowls of geraniums, contains a rose garden, beautifully

Scotland

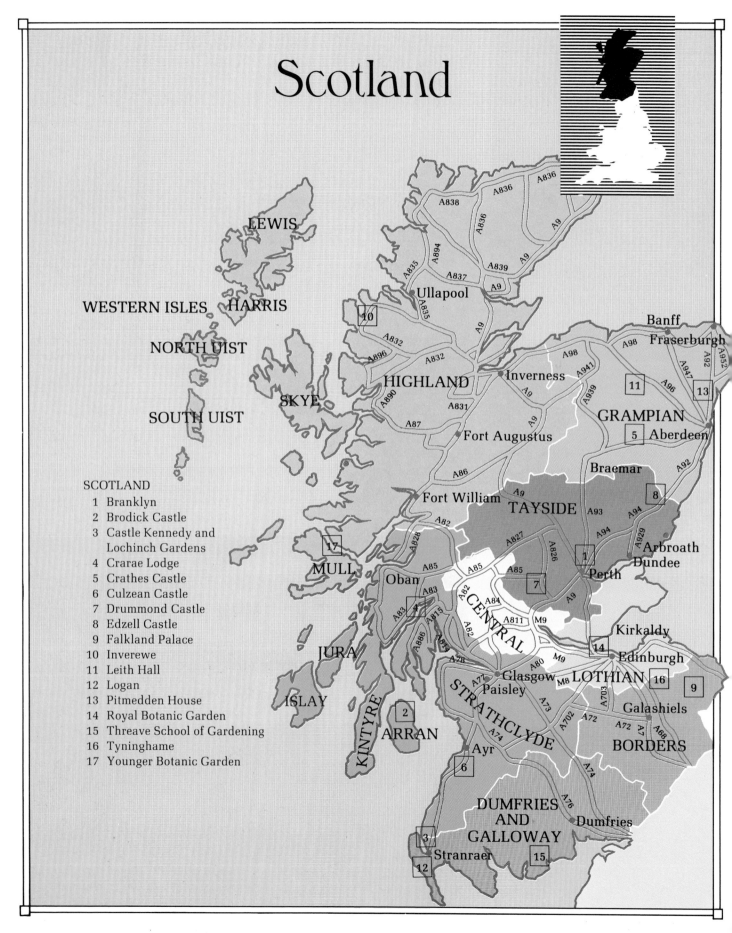

LEWIS

WESTERN ISLES

HARRIS

NORTH UIST

SKYE

SOUTH UIST

Ullapool

HIGHLAND

Inverness

Fort Augustus

Fort William

Banff

Fraserburgh

GRAMPIAN

Aberdeen

Braemar

TAYSIDE

Arbroath

Dundee

Perth

MULL

Oban

CENTRAL

JURA

Kirkaldy

Edinburgh

LOTHIAN

Glasgow

Paisley

Galashiels

ISLAY

KINTYRE

ARRAN

STRATHCLYDE

BORDERS

Ayr

Dumfries

DUMFRIES
AND
GALLOWAY

Stranraer

SCOTLAND

1 Branklyn
2 Brodick Castle
3 Castle Kennedy and
  Lochinch Gardens
4 Crarae Lodge
5 Crathes Castle
6 Culzean Castle
7 Drummond Castle
8 Edzell Castle
9 Falkland Palace
10 Inverewe
11 Leith Hall
12 Logan
13 Pitmedden House
14 Royal Botanic Garden
15 Threave School of Gardening
16 Tyninghame
17 Younger Botanic Garden

104

·1·
BRANKLYN
Perth, Perthshire

The late John and Dorothy Renton had little experience but considerable interest and enthusiasm for plants when they created their small garden in 1926, concentrating first on alpines and heather. Today, maintained by the National Trust for Scotland, it covers about 0.08 hectares (2 acres) and contains a wonderful variety of peat-loving plants in scree beds separated by winding grass paths. Fine trees and shrubs, including magnificent rhodo-dendrons, especially dwarf varieties, form the background to this remarkable garden where everything has been lovingly and carefully selected and allotted its appropriate position in the overall scheme. The place is particularly beautiful in early summer when the rhododendrons, lilies, meconopses, iris and roses are in full bloom, but the alpines and ground cover plants add special interest to this original garden.

Open March to Oct., daily. NT

·2·
BRODICK CASTLE
Isle of Arran

The castle stands on the east side of the Isle of Arran, sheltered from Atlantic gales, and the garden plants benefit from the mild conditions provided by the Gulf Stream. The lovely woodland garden, with its rocks and streams, was created by the Duchess of Montrose, who bequeathed it to the National Trust for Scotland in 1958. It is particularly famous for its fine large-leaved rhododendrons from the Himalayas, China and Burma, which do so well that they seed themselves. The formal walled garden dates back some 250 years and has been restored as a Victorian garden with herbaceous perennials, roses, fuchsias, etc. The rock and water garden is also a comparatively recent addition. Plants from all over the world include tree ferns, acacias, eucryphias, crinodendrons, primulas and many other rare and interesting species. A country park was established in 1980.

Open all year, daily. NT

Crarae Lodge.

·3·
CASTLE KENNEDY AND LOCHINCH GARDENS
Stranraer, Wigtown

Castle Kennedy, seat of the Earls of Stair, was burned down in 1716 and replaced almost 150 years later by Lochinch Castle, 1.6km (1 mile) away. The gardens lie on a peninsula between two lochs, the main one being attached to the ruins of the older castle. This was originally formal in design, with terraces, pool and canal; later it was laid out with avenues and planted with trees. During the 19th century the introduction of exotic trees and shrubs resulted in a change of style until the whole garden was planted to give colour throughout spring and summer. The avenue of monkey puzzle trees dating from 1849 and running from the circular pool to Lochinch Castle is unrivalled in Britian, and there are many other fine specimen trees from that period. The Lochinch garden, hedged and walled, consists of lawns, flower beds and shrub borders.

Open April to Sept., daily.

·4·
CRARAE LODGE
Minard by Inveraray, Argyll

No better site could be imagined for a "natural" garden than this hillside setting where a stream tumbles down through a rock gorge into the waters of Loch Fyne. Climate and soil are ideal, and Sir George Campbell needed to modify it very little when, in the early 1930s, he adapted it for his marvellous collection of exotic trees and shrubs. The woodland is crisscrossed by narrow paths through the trees and banks of shrubs. There are rare firs, pines and cypresses, eucryphias, embothriums and many eucalyptus species; and the magnificent rhododendrons, both small-and large-leaved, and deciduous azaleas provide a continuous canopy of colour in May-June.

Open all year, daily.

·5·
CRATHES CASTLE
Banchory, Kincardine and Deeside

The grey stone castle of Crathes, with its turrets, gables and parapets, dates back to the reign of Mary, Queen of Scots in the 16th century. Situated in woodland high over the River Dee, it is a fascinating place to visit and it is further embellished by one of the most original and lovely gardens in northern Scotland.

This garden, however, is comparatively modern, having been designed, from 1932 onward, by Lady Burnett, wife of Sir James Burnett, and subsequently maintained by the National Trust for Scotland. The original formal garden was planted in 1702, and some of the yew hedges and lime trees are from that period. The hedges now divide up the individual small gardens which lie at the foot of the castle walls. Each of these eight gardens is distinct, with its own character and colour scheme, but they amalgamate most skilfully to form an overall pattern of great beauty. Fine topiary specimens, hedges, neat paths and lawns contribute to the decorative effect, but the main interest and attraction of the garden is in the plants, many of them rare, and the imaginative way in which they have been used. One of the small gardens near the house contains rectangles of clipped yew around a pool and beds planted in shades of red, purple and bronze; a larger one, with a fountain, is predominantly blue and purple; and a third is a yellow garden, with shrubs and herbaceous plants ranging from lime green to orange.

Thanks to a favourable microclimate many unusual and sometimes difficult plants flourish here, and the castle approaches and avenues, too, exhibit a number of rare trees. The greenhouses are also exceptionally well stocked with tender species.

Garden open all year, daily. NT

· 6 ·

CULZEAN CASTLE
Maybole, Ayr

The National Trust for Scotland owns and maintains the castle, its garden and the country park, first in Scotland (1969), which has been developed as a recreation centre, with nature trails. Despite its appearance, it was never a castle proper, but a castellated house redesigned by Robert Adam in elegant Georgian style. The woodland garden remains semi-wild, and the most interesting plants are in the formal fountain garden, with terraces and herbaceous borders, and the walled garden, which contains a grotto and is approached by way of a Victorian camellia house.

Open all year, daily. NT

· 7 ·

DRUMMOND CASTLE
Crieff, Perthshire

For visitors who enter Drummond Castle through its 15th-century keep and paved courtyard, the sight of the great parterre (laid out in the first half of the 19th century) at the foot of a stone staircase comes as a breathtaking surprise. It is on the site of a much older garden and covers some 5.25 hectares (13 acres), its size and complexity of design being quite astonishing. It is in the form of an immense cross, with trees, topiary specimens, lawns, flower beds and statues; and in the centre is a tall 17th-century sundial with some 50 separate faces. Beyond the parterre, over a stream and up a slight slope, is a broad grass ride through woodland.

Open April to Sept.; May to Aug. daily, otherwise Wed. and Sun.

Far left: *Culzean Castle.*
Left: *Edzell Castle.*

• 8 •
EDZELL CASTLE
Edzell, Angus

The castle is a ruin but the little walled garden is a gem, reconstructed in the 1930s to reproduce as accurately as possible the formal garden originally made by Sir David Lindsay in 1604. It is rectangular and completely enclosed by red sandstone walls, one of them that of the ruined castle itself. The walls are divided into panels and decorated with a chequered pattern of niches (scooped out for flower boxes) and carved figures with an opening below for flowers. Larger niches along the top of the walls may have been intended for busts and urns, and there are also nesting holes for birds. The whole pattern is geometrical, with flower beds and trimmed box, and a red sandstone pavilion stands in one corner.

Open all year, daily except Tues., Thurs. mornings.

• 9 •
FALKLAND PALACE
Falkland, Fife

This lovely building, partially in ruins but partially residential, was once owned by the widow of James II of Scotland and was a hunting palace of the Stuart monarchs. The present garden, maintained by the National Trust for Scotland and largely made by Percy Cane, dates from 1945, and consists essentially of lawns and island beds, planted with trees, shrubs and hardy perennials, with one big herbaceous border backed by a wall with roses and other climbers. A courtyard with water lilies and flower borders flanks the indoor royal tennis court, dating from 1539. There is also a heather garden and a rose garden. Terraces, paths and formal areas are neatly and attractively laid out to blend with the palace walls and ruins.

Open April to Sept., daily. NT

• 10 •
INVEREWE
Poolewe, Ross, Cromarty and Skye

This lovely garden, containing one of the most remarkable collections of rare and delicate plants in Britain, is located on what appeared to be a most unpromising site. In 1862 Osgood Mackenzie purchased this rocky peninsula on the north-west coast of Scotland. Jutting out into a sea loch, the ground was virtually bare of vegetation and the little soil that existed was black peat. Additional good soil had to be brought to the site in baskets, and as shelter against gales a belt of trees, mainly Corsican pine and Scots fir, but also other conifers, was planted. Over the years woodland gradually covered the entire peninsula, and it became possible to plant an enormous range of trees and shrubs, including silver birches and rhododendrons. A century later, thanks to a mild climate and the fact that most of the species, both native and foreign, have been allowed to grow naturally, Inverewe, now owned by the National Trust for Scotland, is a showplace of exceptional interest and beauty, particularly in spring and early summer. Specialities include rhododendrons, celmisias, meconopses and primulas, and there is an excellent guide which lists the principal plants.

The area in front of the simple white house consists of lawn, herbaceous borders, a rock wall and a rock bank. Elsewhere it is a woodland setting, with winding paths and steps. One section is an enclosure amusingly called Bambooselem, which contains tender plants, flowering trees (including a spectacular *Magnolia campbellii*) and, predictably, dense plantings of bamboos.

Garden open all year, daily. NT

• 11 •
LEITH HALL
Kennethmont, Aberdeen

The National Trust for Scotland administers this garden, situated some distance away from the 17th-century mansion. It consists essentially of zigzag herbaceous borders and a rock garden planted mainly with herbaceous perennials. There are masses of flowers everywhere, and the extensive grounds beyond the garden provide ample scope for pleasant countryside walks.

Open all year, daily. NT

• 12 •
LOGAN
Port Logan by Stranraer, Wigtown

This beautiful garden benefits from an exceptionally mild climate because of its southerly situation and proximity to the sea. The Royal Botanic Garden has therefore grown plants here, both in the open and in walled enclosures, which do not normally flourish outdoors in Britain, giving it something of a Mediterranean atmosphere. The woodland area contains rare rhododendrons, magnolias, camellias, meconopses, etc. and in the water garden there are cabbage palms (an avenue of these stands beside a pool) and several species of tree fern. It is a marvellous collection of exotic plants in a lovely setting.

Open April to Sept., daily.

·13·
PITMEDDEN HOUSE
Pitmedden, Aberdeen

Here the National Trust for Scotland has reconstructed the Great Garden laid out in the 17th century for Sir Alexander Seton, employing the same designer as for the similar, though smaller, parterre at Edzell Castle. The formal garden at Pitmedden consists of four large parterres enclosed by three terraces and a wall, and has two hand-

some gazebos. Since there were no plans of the original garden, new designs had to be made in 1952, three of them modelled on the gardens of Holyroodhouse, Edinburgh, the fourth on Sir Alexander Seton's coat-of-arms. The parterres are filled with flowering annuals and outlined in box hedges, and a double row of yew cones runs down the centre. Visitors can also enjoy farming and garden displays, and other entertainments.

Open all year, daily. NT

· 14 ·
ROYAL BOTANIC GARDEN
Edinburgh, West Lothian

The magnificent rock garden here is one of the finest in the British Isles, and peat beds permit an exceptionally wide range of plants to be grown. There are

many splendid trees and shrubs, including fine rhododendrons. In 1967 a new plant house was built as an adjunct to the two Victorian palm houses already there. This greenhouse is similar to, but much larger than, the one at Chatsworth, its weight suspended by exterior steel cables to give unimpeded space inside, and it includes a tank for tropical aquatic plants.

Open all year, daily.

· 15 ·
THREAVE SCHOOL OF GARDENING
Castle Douglas, Stewartry

Since 1957 the National Trust for Scotland has developed a private estate into a school of gardening. Apart from a walled garden, a kitchen garden and small woodland areas, the island bed principle has been used throughout for herbaceous plants, roses, shrubs, rock plants and heathers. The unified rock and peat gardens are particularly well planted and there is a pool for moisture-loving species and aquatics. Apart from its practical function, Threave is a delightful place at any season.

Open all year, daily. NT

· 16 ·
TYNINGHAME
Dunbar, East Lothian

Tyninghame, a castellated building in red sandstone, has belonged to the Earls of Haddington since 1624. The large garden has undergone many changes over the centuries, but although some ancient trees, including a triple avenue of beech, still survive, nothing remains of the 18th-century pattern of straight alleys and rides, and the rather stiff formality of the Victorian garden, with its gravel paths, lawns and flower beds, has been transformed by Lord and Lady Haddington since 1952.

The Victorian parterre to the east of

Far left: *Logan.*
Above and left: *Edinburgh, Royal Botanic Garden.*

the house, with a tall sundial in the centre, has been replanted with roses, shrubs and herbaceous perennials; and beyond it is a delightful enclosed garden with plants entirely chosen by Lady Haddington, particularly old-fashioned and shrub roses, but also lilies and hardy perennials. The planting is informal, yet firmly controlled. There is a trelliswork arbour with a statue of Flora, and on either side of the iron entrance gate are brick piers with statues of children.

Away from the house, through woodland with banks of rhododendrons and azaleas, is the old walled kitchen garden, with wide turf paths, box-edged flower beds and high yew hedges fronted by statues. The fountain in the centre is decorated with horses' heads. Outside the walled garden is a pleached alley of apple trees dating from the late 19th century. There is also an attractive heather garden.

Situated so close to the sea, Tyninghame enjoys mild winters, ideal for the profusion of flowers, shrubs and trees that make this garden so attractive.

Garden open June to Sept., weekdays.

Ulster

IRELAND
1 Castlewellan
2 Mount Stewart
3 Rowallane

·17·
YOUNGER BOTANIC GARDEN
Benmore, nr Dunoon, Argyll

This lovely woodland garden in a wild mountain and river setting is an annexe of the Edinburgh Royal Botanic Garden, established because of its moist climate specifically for conifers and flowering shrubs. The avenue of wellingtonias leading up to the house is unrivalled in Britain, and the collection of rhododendrons, in bloom from early in the year until late summer, is exceptional. An impressive formal feature is the main lawn, enclosed on three sides by walls, and its elegant pavilion.

Open April to Oct., daily.

·1·
CASTLEWELLAN
nr Newcastle, Co. Down

The walled arboretum, the park around the lake, and the woods behind contain a spendid collection of trees planted just over a century ago, which include both conifers and broad-leaved species. The rhododendrons, azaleas and other flowering shrubs are exceptionally fine.

Open all year, daily.

·2·
MOUNT STEWART
Co. Down

The Marchioness of Londonderry left her impact on the garden she created between the wars, both in terms of planting and design. A mild climate encouraged the growth of many semi-tender species and the luxurance and variety of planting that she promoted has been perpetuated by the National

Trust since 1955. Her individual taste and sense of humour is also reflected in much of the decoration of her modern garden. Distinct from this newer garden is an 18th-century landscape with a lake and two-storey Temple of the Winds. Lady Londonderry's garden includes an Italian-style terrace, a large sunken garden, a shamrock-shaped topiary garden, a wild garden and a flower garden in the pattern of a rose around a fountain. There are numerous garden ornaments in the form of animals, some of them caricaturing her friends, and a hedge in the topiary garden represents a hunt in which the stag is saved by the devil. Elsewhere there is a heather pattern of the red hand of Ulster. The garden is thus rich in botanical interest and contains many other unusual pleasures.

Open April to Sept., daily except Tues. NT

· 3 ·
ROWALLANE
Saintfield, Co. Down

The broad drive by which the visitor approaches the house, flanked by great beeches, Scots pines, wellingtonias and rhododendrons, is an indication that this is a place where shrubs and trees are to be found in rich abundance. Yet it gives something of a misleading impression, for Rowallane, with its extraordinary collection of plants, many of them tender and rare, has an originality and individuality that is unique. The name is derived from a Celtic word for "rocky outcrop", and this is indeed one of the garden's most striking features, largely determining its nature from the moment when Hugh Armytage Moore began to lay it out and

plant it in 1903. His uncle, the Rev. John Moore, had planted a kitchen garden inside walls with pierced tiles to carry wires for training fruit trees, but all the rest was his own work. Apart from the formal sections near the house, the present garden is a mixture of semi-wilderness and woodland, having spilled over in places into the adjoining fields, the separate areas being divided by low stone walls with gates and stiles. Although the original soil was poor, and had to be supplemented by the cartload, the scattered smooth outcrops of rock proved ideal for making the rock gardens which are such a delightful feature of the garden today. But Mr Moore was also an enthusiastic and skilled plantsman, raising many unusual and foreign species from seed and creating hybrids of his own.

Examples of such specialities, both of which received awards, are *Viburnum plicatum* "Rowallane" and *Chaenomeles superba* "Rowallane".

The garden is perhaps at its best in late spring when the rhododendrons and azaleas are in full bloom, but there is an abundance of colour at all seasons, in the Spring Garden, the Walled Garden and in the natural, informal areas. Although Rowallane was somewhat neglected in the post-war years, it has been magnificently maintained since 1955 by the National Trust.

Garden open all year, daily. NT

Castlewellan, arboretum.

Index

Credits

BRITISH TOURIST AUTHORITY
11, 18, 30, 30–31, 37T, 38B, 46, 47, 64, 65 and jacket, 67, 71, 76, 77, 80, 88–89, 91, 95, 99, 103, 111.

JERRY COLLINS
8–9, 26–27, 36, 43, 50, 62, 70, 78, 86, 90–91, 104, 110

MARTIN DOHRN
10, 12–16, 23–25, 28, 29, 37B, 38–39, 40, 41, 42, 86–87.

KELLY FLYNN
28–29, 31, 33, 34, 35, and back jacket.

JERRY HARPUR
61

SUE LINES
14, 21, 24, 30, 35, 41, 44, 53, 56, 69, 72, 83, 89, 96, 101

NICK MEERS
51–60, 79

CERI NORMAN
43, 48, 49, 87

JOHN RILEY
19–21, 63, 66–67, 68, 69, 72–75, 82–85, 92.

SCOTTISH TOURIST BOARD
105–109

HANS VERKROOST
27

DAVID WARD
44, 45, 93, 94, 96, 97, 100–103

T = Top B = Bottom